World Economic Review
Volume 3, 2014

Table of Contents

The *World Economic Review* is an open-access journal published by the World Economics Association in line with its commitment to: rigorous economic research; pluralism in the approaches to economic analysis; openness in the procedures and processes; inclusivity of access; and ethical behaviour.

We publish articles in all branches, methods, and paradigmatic approaches of economics, except those related to the history of economic thought, philosophy and methodology for which the WEA has the dedicated journal *Economic Thought*. Articles with a multidisciplinary content are welcome.

The *World Economic Review* aims to promote economics' engagement with the real world so as to confront, explain, and make tractable economic phenomena.

Website http://wer.worldeconomicsassociation.org
Contact wereditor@worldeconomicsassociation.org

© Individual authors, WEA and College Publications 2014.
All rights reserved.

ISSN 2055-6322 (print)
ISSN 2049-3517 (online)
ISBN 978-1-84890-152-0

Published by College Publications on behalf of the World Economics Association
Sister WEA open-access journals: *Economic Thought* and *Real-World Economics Review*

College Publications
Scientific Director: Dov Gabbay
Managing Director: Jane Spurr

http://www.collegepublications.co.uk

Original cover design WEA.
Printed by Lightning Source, Milton Keynes, UK

The Evolution of Economic Inequality in the United States, 1969-2012: Evidence from Data on Inter-industrial Earnings and Inter-regional Incomes

James K. Galbraith and J. Travis Hale[1]

LBJ School of Public Affairs, University of Texas, USA

Abstract

This paper provides measures of earnings inequality in the United States across economic sectors, measured within states, from 1969 through 2012, and of income inequality across counties, from 1969 through 2007. These measures permit detailed decomposition of changes in inequality, highlighting the major gainers and losers in relative terms. They illustrate the roles played by the financial sector, by the technology boom, by war-time public spending and by the real estate bubble in driving the evolution of economic inequality in the United States.

Between-industry earnings inequality in the United States

In 1955 Simon Kuznets postulated that industrialization first increases inequality because factories pay more than farms, but that inequality later declines as the weight of agriculture in the employment mix drops. Thus in Kuznets' simple model there are two sources of inequality: the difference in average wages between farms and factories, and the distribution of the population across these sectors. A reduction of either sector or of the differential will decrease the inequality measured between sectors.[2] The famous inverted-U hypothesis is mainly based on inter-sectoral transitions in the process of economic development, as the balance of workers in the two sectors first increases and then declines.

In the complex modern U.S. economy we can measure changing earnings inequality using the same principles. Overall inequality measured across sectors depends on the differentials between average wages by sector and on their comparative size. As

---

[1] Authors' contact information: Galbraith@mail.utexas.edu, jtravishale@gmail.com
[2] Kuznets was not interested in inequalities stemming from non-labor sources of income, such as capital gains, and excluded them from his analysis to avoid undue complications. Our sector analysis follows Kuznets in being based on payrolls; however the geographic analysis is based on income tax returns and so includes capital gains and other forms of unearned income.

the work of Conceição, Galbraith and Bradford (2001) shows, classification schemes that break the economy into a relatively small number of sectors often capture the major dimensions of pay variability. Economic sectors are a particularly sensitive fault line – the relative fortunes of sectors capture many important economic changes. With sectoral data, for instance, it is true that pay inequalities among individuals *within* particular firms and industries are not captured. But while these inequalities are substantial, they tend (partly for institutional reasons, such as the stability of intra-firm pay hierarchies) to vary less, over time, than the inequalities between sectors. So even a coarse, sector-level disaggregation often captures most of the changes that occur.

Method and measurement

The Bureau of Economic Analysis (BEA) publishes annual earnings and employment data for industrial sectors the nation as the whole and for individual states. Earnings are defined as "the sum of Wage and Salary Disbursements, supplements to wages and salaries and proprietors' income" and derive from a virtual census of employers' tax records. (BEA 2008). As such, there is almost complete coverage of the (formal) working population with minimal reporting error.

From 1969 until 2000, data were organized according to the Standard Industrial Classification (SIC) coding system. Beginning in 2001, the BEA dropped the SIC schema in favor of the North American Industry Classification System (NAICS). To ease comparisons between the two taxonomies, the BEA released recoded data for the 1990 to 2000 period using the NAICS categories. Thus, there are two annual datasets with a decade of overlap, one from 1969 to 2000 and the other from 1990 to 2012.

Many of the standard inequality metrics can be used to describe the distribution of pay; we focus on Theil's T in our calculations. Given the wage bills and employment levels for a mutually exclusive and completely exhaustive set of industries, Theil's T is:

$$T'_{Sectors} = \sum_{i=1}^{m} \frac{p_i}{P} * \frac{y_i}{\mu} * \ln(\frac{y_i}{\mu})$$

where p_i is the number of jobs in sector i, P is the total number of jobs in the United States, y_i is the average pay in sector i, and μ is the average pay for all jobs. We refer to the terms within the summation sign, one for each category, as "Theil elements." As with

Kuznets' hypothesis, inter-sectoral pay inequality is a function of the relative size of the sectors and of their relative wages.

In addition to measuring inequality between sectors, Theil's T Statistic allows us to identify those sectors most responsible for changing inequality. By examining the Theil elements, we can isolate the contribution of each sector to total inequality between sectors. The Theil element will be positive or negative, depending on whether the sector's average earnings are greater or less than the national average, with the contribution weighted by sector size. By construction, the sum of the positive elements must be greater than the sum of the negative elements.

An attractive property of Theil's T is decomposability. Given two or more groups, total inequality is made up of two components, a between-group component (T'_g) and a within-groups component (T''_g), each of them always positive, and the latter a weighted sum of the inequalities measured inside each group.

$$T = T'_g + T''_g$$

As a moment's reflection will confirm, expanding the number of groups transfers inequality from the within-groups component to the between-groups component, so that T'_g grows and becomes a closer approximation of total inequality as the group structure becomes more fine. However, if we are correct in thinking that between-sector movements dominate the evolution of inequality, it should not be necessary to disaggregate too much, before the major movements in the structure of incomes over time become clear. In practice, Theil's T measured across fairly coarse group structures is a simple, inexpensive, and robust way to calculate and track the movement of economic inequalities through time.

The evolution of between-sector earnings inequality

Figure 1 displays *earnings inequality* calculated on the SIC basis from 1969 to 1990 and the NAICS basis from 1990 to 2012 (authors' calculations from BEA data) and Census Bureau measures of household *income inequality* over a similar period (DeNavas-Walt et al. 2008). These earnings inequality measures are based on a relatively fine disaggregation of sectors-within-states -- that is oil drilling in Texas compared to farming in Utah compared to retail in Rhode Island compared to all the other combinations of states and sectors.

Earnings inequality rose substantially over the period observed, but the rate of change varied. From 1969 to 1982, the between state-sector measure of Theil's T increased 61%, but following the sharp rise in the recessions of the early 1980s, earnings inequality remained flat until 1994. There was another run-up in the late 1990s, coinciding with the information-technology boom, and then again in the 2000s.

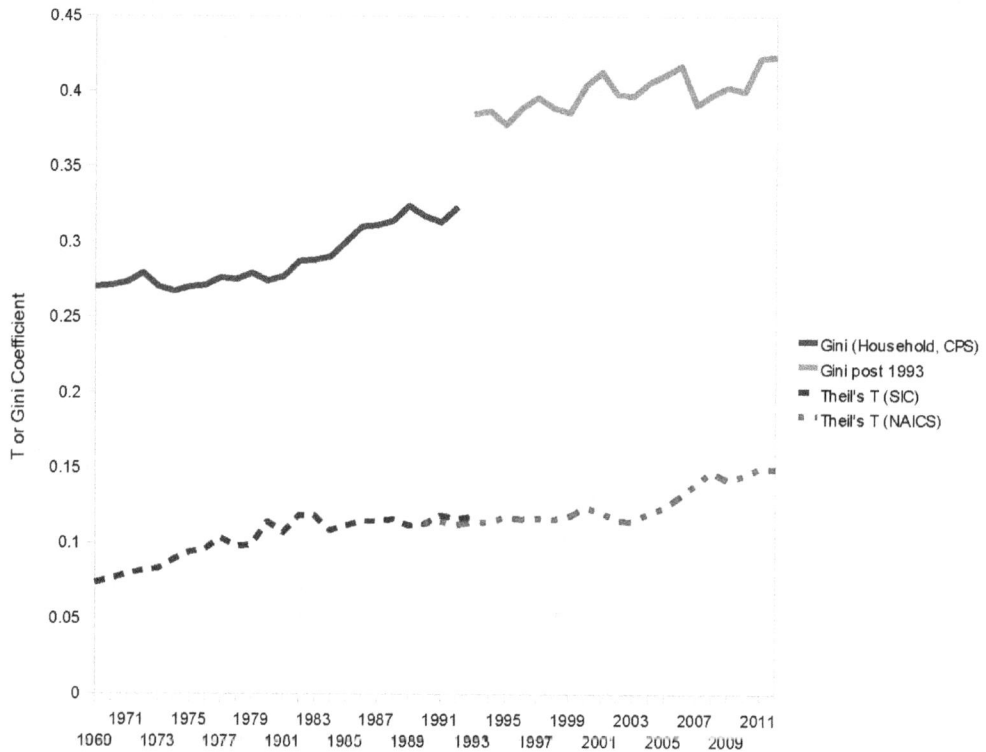

Figure 1. Between State-Sector Earnings Inequality and Household Income Inequality 1969–2012[3]

The shift in coding regimes from SIC to NAICS has little effect on the pay inequality metric. On the other hand, the CPS-based household income inequality measure has a major data break in the early 1990s (apparently related to the revised treatment of top-coding), as the figure shows. When this is adjusted for, the two series show approximately similar rates of change through time, though year-to-year fluctuations do vary.

---

[3] A change in top-coding values and survey methodology accounts for the break in the Gini series between 1992 and 1993.

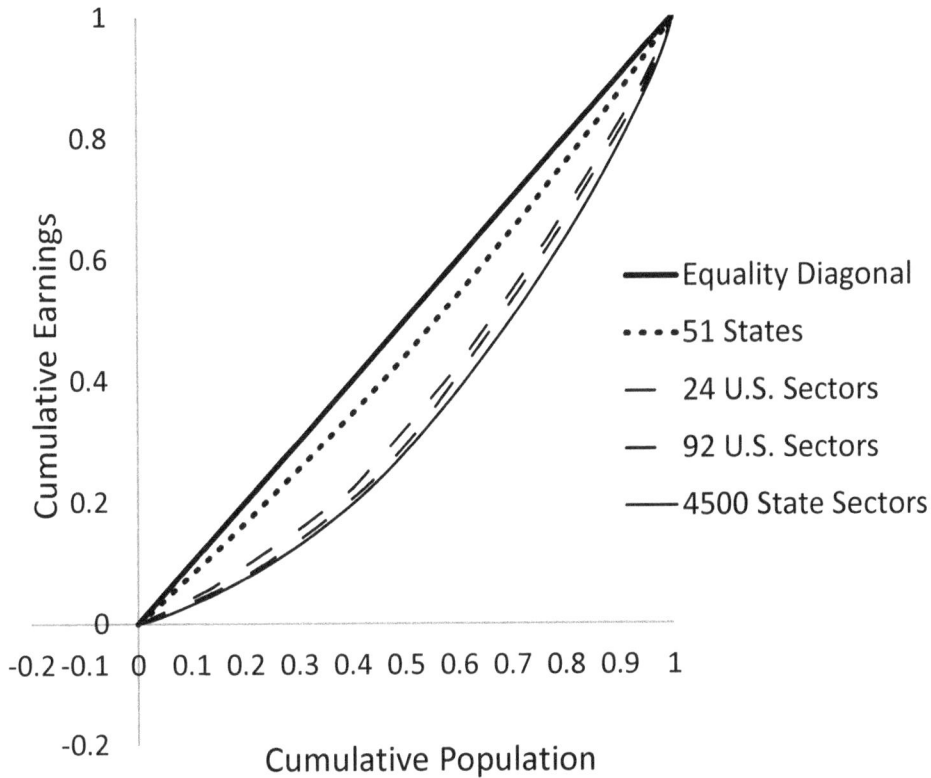

Figure 2. Lorenz Curves for the U.S. Distribution of Pay in 2012 Using Various Group Structures

The richness of the BEA data allows us to explore pay inequality through a myriad of lenses – broader or narrower sectorizations at the state and the national level. Figure 2 displays Lorenz Curves for 4 different group structures in 2007: 51 states (all sectors combined), 21 national sectors, 93 national sectors, and 4389 (very narrow) sectors-within-states.[4]

Each of these Lorenz curves has an associated Gini coefficient – 51 States: 0.089; 21 National Sectors: 0.259; 93 National Sectors: 0.301; 4389 State Sectors: 0.320. As one adds detail, of course inequality increases. The graphs and Gini

---

[4] We variously treat Washington D.C. as a state- and a county-equivalent depending on the context. The Appendix lists the available NAICS-based sectors.

coefficients also show that in the United States, sector matters more than state. There is greater inequality in pay *between* industries, even at a fairly coarse level of disaggregation, than *between* states. Second, adding sector detail or combining state detail with the sector detail provides little additional information – the set of 21 national sectors captures the bulk of between-state-sector pay differences and the set of 93 national sectors captures almost all of it.

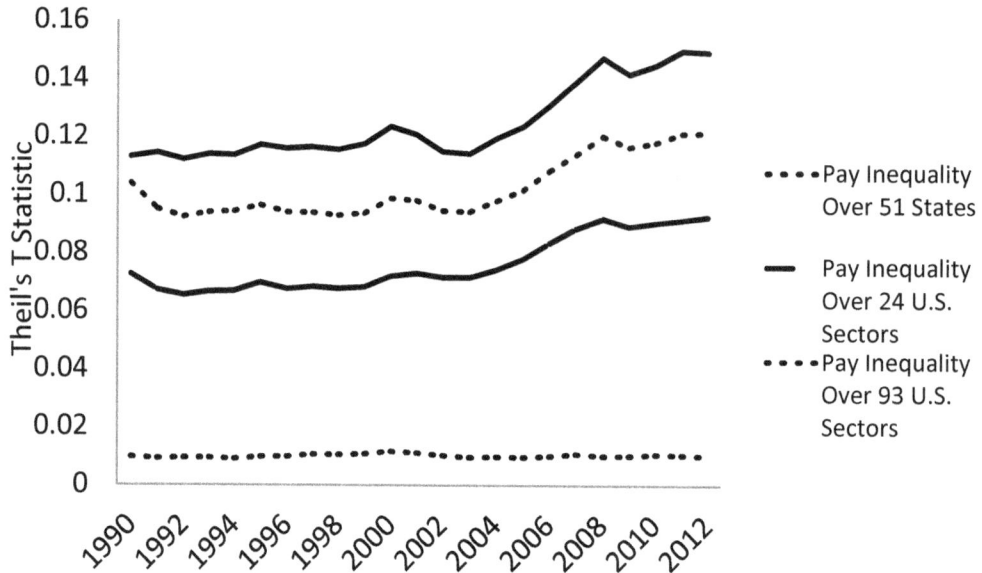

Figure 3. U.S. Pay Inequality 1990 to 20012 Calculated Using Alternative Category Structures

Figure 3 displays the evolution of pay inequality from 1990 to 2012 using the same four category structures. The different measures move together over time, which shows that it is not necessary to disaggregate in order to capture time-variation. Yet each between-sector metric is useful in its own way. The 21-sector national measure is easier to visualize, while the more detailed measures help to identify those narrow groups most responsible for changes.

Figure 4 breaks down the annual measures of pay inequality among the 21 broad national sectors into their constituent Theil Elements. The black line tracks the Theil's T, while the stacked portions of the bar graphs show the Theil elements. From the zero line upward, the major contributors to inequality are manufacturing, professional scientific and technical services, management of companies and enterprises, federal civilian government, wholesale trade, information, local government, and finance and insurance – the last being the volatile large blocks toward the top of the diagram[5]. From the zero line downward, retail trade, accommodation, other services, waste management and real estate are the leading lower-income sectors. Health care occupies a thin line just at the zero line: health is a large sector, but with average earnings just at the national average, and therefore little net effect on inequality.

Several trends emerge clearly. One is the rise of professional, scientific and technical services in the information-technology boom through 2000. Another is the waning of the public sector, both federal and local, from 1990 to 2000 and then its recovery as a significant contributor to inequality in the early 2000s. It is notable that the Democratic years under Presidents Clinton and Obama were not banner ones for government; this sector fared better under the Republicans. A third trend is the rising importance of finance and insurance during the boom years from 1990 until 2001 but even more so during the run up to the financial crisis in 2007. Thereafter, the relative weight of the financial sector shrinks – and overall inequality also declined a bit. Taken as a whole, the period from 1990 to 2012 was one of rising earnings inequality, with a peak in 2000 and again in 2007. Inequality then subsides, but quickly recovers and by 2012 it was near or at its previous peak.

---

[5] Finance and insurance is shown in orange in the color version of the graphic.

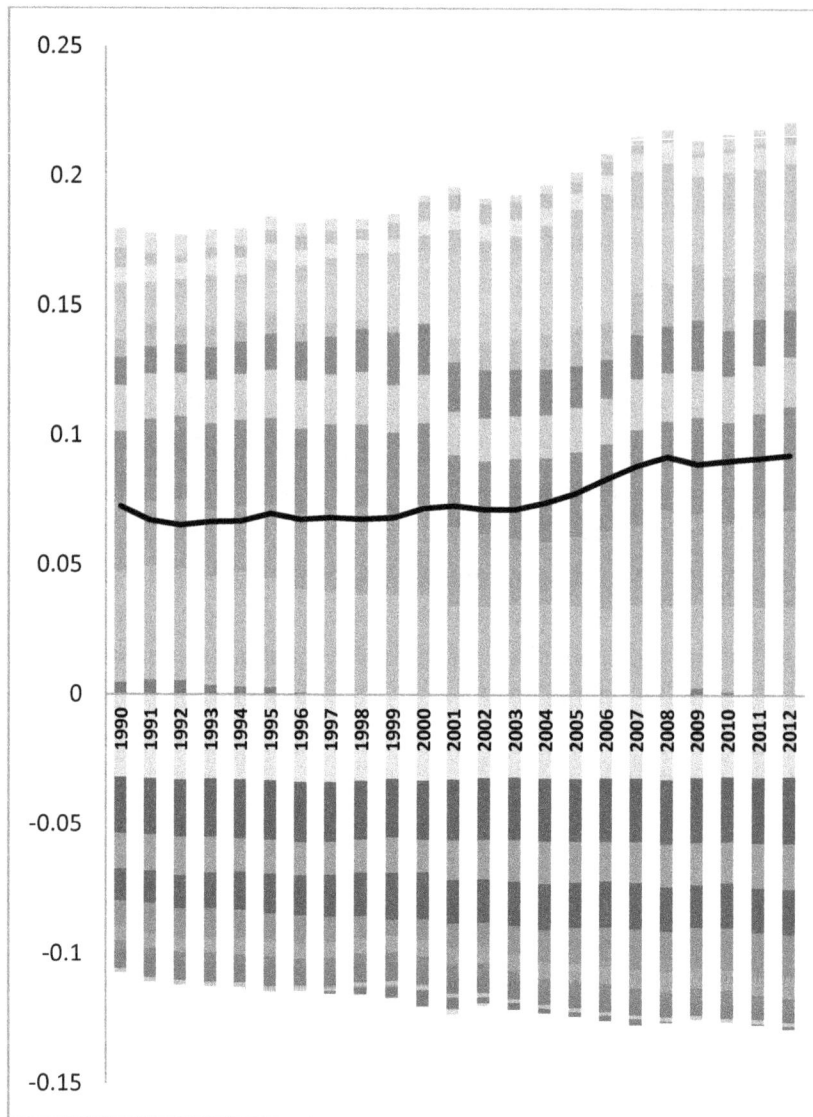

Figure 4. Theil Elements of Between-Sector Pay Inequality in the U.S. 1990 – 2012

As Kuznets taught, the source of increasing inequality may be either changes in relative wages or changes in sector employment shares. Though a massive contributor to inequality, finance and insurance saw a slight decline in jobs over this period. Its contribution to rising inequality came from strong (though variable) growth in relative earnings. Professional and technical services, spurred (as noted) by the information technology revolution, gained employment share and also experienced a small increase

8

in relative earnings. Manufacturing, a high-wage sector, maintained or improved its relative wage position but lost employment. Administrative and waste services and real estate rental and leasing, which both experienced significant employment gains, added the most to growing inequality from below. Relative average earnings in real estate actually improved, which would tend to reduce inequality, but not enough to offset the flood of new jobs into what remains a low-paid sector.

Winners and losers during the information-technology and beltway booms

When we expand the number of sectors subject to analysis, from 21 to 93 and beyond, we find that only a small handful of sub-sectors, with a very small minority of the nation's workforce, account for the most significant changes in pay inequality observed at this time.

Common sense can guide the search for these high-impact sectors. The emergence of personal computing and information technology as major forces in the mid- to late 1990s and the mortgage-finance bubble of the mid 2000s were the hallmark economic phenomena of those times. From 1996 to 2000, for example, nominal earnings per reported job in computer and electronics manufacturing rose from $57,268 to $83,848. From 2001 to 2006, earnings per job for construction of buildings grew from $53,140 to $66,112, *and* the sector added more than 300,000 jobs. For these reasons, computer manufacturing and construction were significant contributors to the increase in earnings inequality during these episodes. Other sectors saw comparably wide swings in their fortunes, but it turns out that these, taken together, affected only a very small fraction of the total workforce. Thus pay increases in sectors listed in Table 1, which contained only 3.8% of all workers in 2001, account for the entire rise in pay inequality during the late 1990s.

These boom sectors experienced a 58% climb in nominal average earnings in this five year period, while all other sectors gained 22%. The employment growth rate in the high flyers, on the other hand, was roughly half that for the rest of the economy. Thus the separation of the boom sectors from the rest of the economy explains *all* of the increase in between sector inequality from 1991 to 2001. This is evident in Figure 5, which parses Theil's T for between-sector earnings inequality into three components: inequality *among* the IT boom sectors, inequality *among* the sectors in the rest of the economy, and inequality *between* the high-growth sectors and the rest of the economy writ large from 1991 to 2001.

Table 1. Average Earnings in 1996 and 2001 in 12 High-Growth Sectors

Sector	Average Earnings	
	1996	2001
Computer and electronic product manufacturing	$ 57,268	$ 78,198
ISPs, search portals, and data processing	$ 44,426	$ 68,175
International organizations; foreign embassies; consulates	$ 83,632	$ 107,550
Internet publishing and broadcasting	$ 54,116	$ 82,080
Funds, trusts, and other financial vehicles	$ 50,132	$ 79,931
Utilities	$ 82,384	$ 113,605
Oil and gas extraction	$ 49,765	$ 90,958
Broadcasting, except Internet	$ 91,831	$ 133,576
Securities, commodity contracts, investments	$ 46,249	$ 88,604
Petroleum and coal products manufacturing	$ 124,821	$ 200,367
Lessors of nonfinancial intangible assets	$ 91,556	$ 192,836
Pipeline transportation	$ 93,285	$ 299,978
All other Sectors	$ 31,276	$ 38,099

Inequality *between* the boom and the not-boom sectors, taken as groups, is clearly the driving force behind rising inequality overall. Inequality between the 12 sectors in Table 1 that make up the boom sectors was essentially unchanged from 1991 to 2001. Inequality between the other 82 national sectors actually declined a bit. But inequality between the booms and the boom-nots rose significantly, accounting for all of the 17.2% increase in between-sector earnings inequality during this period.

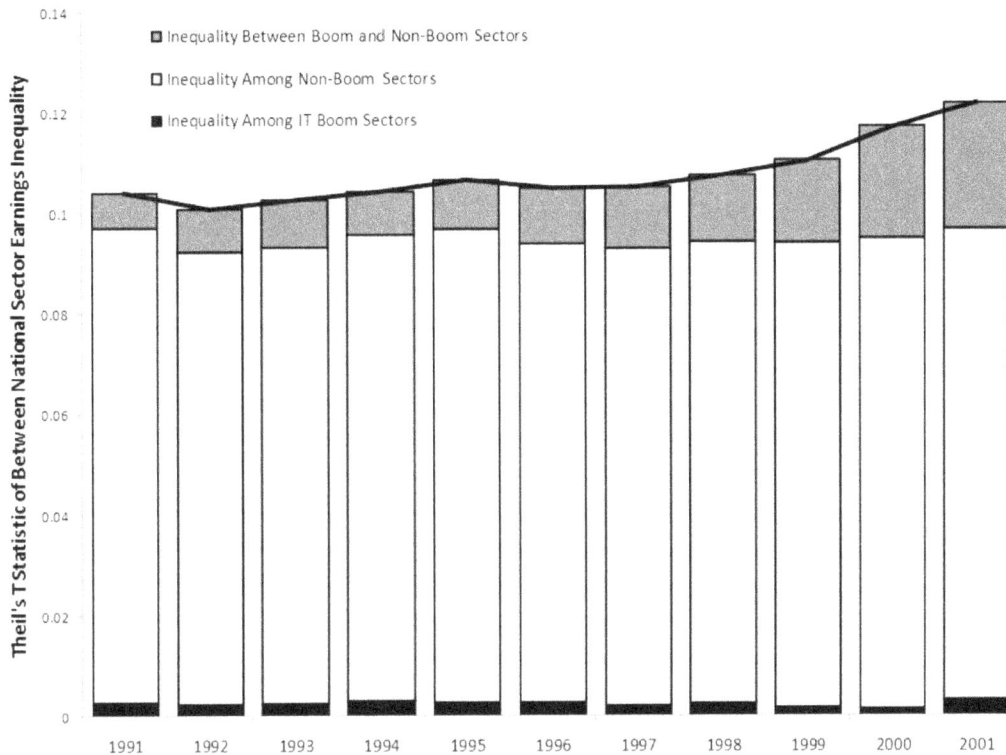

Figure 5. Between-Sector Inequality 1991–2001

The rise in between-sector pay inequality from 2003 to 2007 reflects wage gains in a wider array of sectors that contain a higher percentage of employment, so the gains in those years were more broadly based. But the pattern is similar. Table 2 shows average wages in fifteen high-growth sectors from 2003 to 2007.

These sectors accounted for 7.4% of total jobs in 2007. From 2003 to 2007, average earnings in these "Bush boom" sectors increased 32%, while earnings in the rest of the economy averaged 13%, barely keeping pace with inflation. Once again, the rate of job growth in the high-flyers was half of that for the other sectors. After experiencing brief stagnation in earnings growth during the information-technology bust, computer and electronic product manufacturing and securities, commodity contracts, and investing experienced strong rebounds in earnings from 2002 to 2007. However, neither of these sectors regained the employment levels of 2000. To the contrary, for instance, computer and electronic product manufacturing shed 29% of its workforce from 2000 to 2007.

Table 2. Average Earnings in 2003 and 2007 in 15 High-Growth Sectors

Sector	Average Earnings	
	2003	2007
Military	$ 53,178	$ 71,616
Federal, civilian	$ 79,153	$ 98,844
Computer and electronic product manufacturing	$ 88,365	$ 108,125
Mining (except oil and gas)	$ 66,671	$ 89,371
Water transportation	$ 70,634	$ 93,452
Management of companies and enterprises	$ 83,618	$ 106,587
Support activities for mining	$ 61,650	$ 87,241
Chemical manufacturing	$ 97,062	$ 124,020
Utilities	$ 127,487	$ 157,138
Securities, commodity contracts, investments	$ 83,053	$ 113,907
Broadcasting, except Internet	$ 149,362	$ 197,862
Other information services	$ 34,490	$ 86,726
Oil and gas extraction	$ 98,979	$ 167,418
Pipeline transportation	$ 181,197	$ 263,350
Petroleum and coal products manufacturing	$ 185,070	$ 363,962
All other sectors	$ 38,989	$ 43,949

Figure 6 shows the contributions of inequality among the Bush boom sectors, inequality among all other sectors, and inequality between the high growth sectors and lower-growth sectors from 2000 to 2007.

Unlike the information technology boom, the Bush boom saw rising inequality *among* the boom sectors, *among* the sectors in the rest of the economy, and also *between* those sectors that surged ahead and those that stayed behind. Nonetheless, in this period, as before, the disparity between the booms and boom-nots explains the majority of the total increase in between-sector earnings inequality.

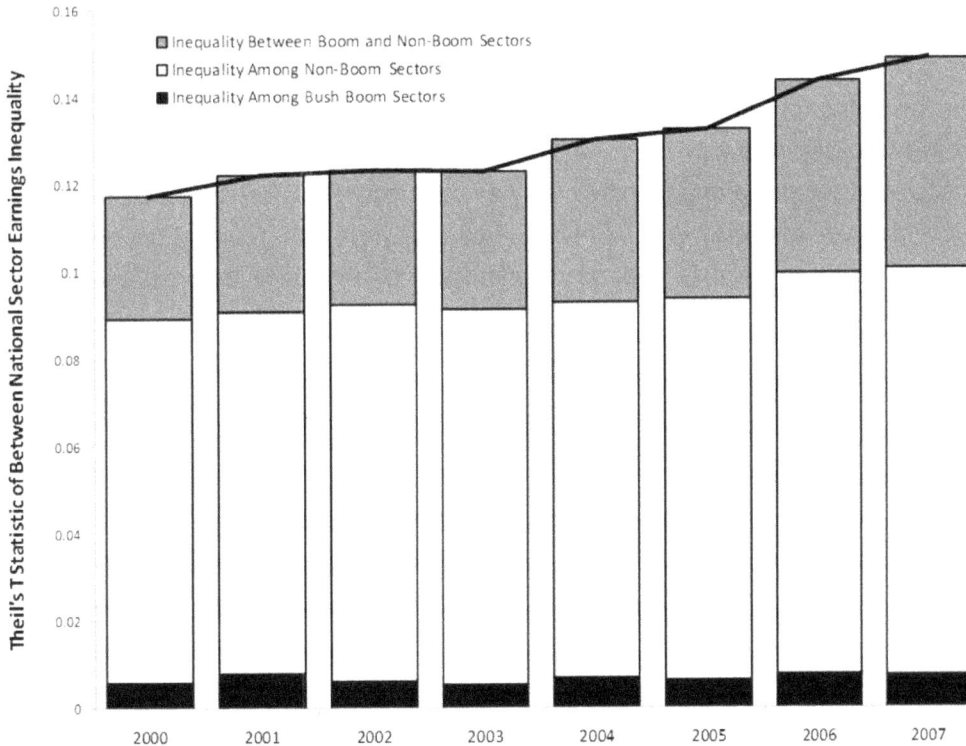

Figure 6. Between-Sector Inequality 2000 –2007

By coincidence or design, sector performance has an apparent political dimension. Bankers and technologists were key supporters of President Clinton; those sectors thrived during his presidency. Under President Bush, workers in extraction industries, the military and government did well, doubtless reflecting the pro-oil and empire-building policies of those years.

The lagging sectors are also informative. In the 2000s, for instance, declining fortunes in the auto industry mitigated the effect on total inequality of expansion and earnings gains in other sectors. The motor vehicles, bodies and trailers, and parts manufacturing sector, which consistently pays high wages, lost jobs and saw stagnant earnings from 2002 to 2007; thus inequality *declined* on that account. This is of course not good news, and sounds a caution against regarding any inequality statistic as *per se* indicative of social welfare.

Education as an inequality remedy?

When public discourse admits inequality to be a problem, education is often given as the cure. According to Treasury Secretary Henry Paulson (2006), for instance, the correct response to rising inequality is to "focus on helping people of all ages pursue first-rate education and retraining opportunities, so they can acquire the skills needed to advance in a competitive worldwide environment." This is a view with powerful support among economists. But the simple inter-sector dynamics show clearly that, as a solution to inequality, education is a bust.

As we've shown, the last two decades have seen significantly *slower* job growth in the high-earnings-growth sectors than in the economy at large. So even if large numbers of young people do "acquire the skills needed to advance" *there is no evidence that the economy will provide them with jobs to suit.* Many will simply end up not using their skills. Moreover, a strategy of investment in education presupposes advance knowledge of *what the education should be for.* Years of education in different fields are not perfect substitutes, and it does little good to train too many people for jobs that, in the short space of four or five years, may (and do) fall out of fashion. And experience shows clearly that the population *does not* know, in advance, *what* to train for. Rather, education and training have become a kind of lottery, whose winners and losers are determined, *ex post*, by the behavior of the economy.

Students who studied information technology in the mid-1990s were lucky; they were a scarce few who could find places easily in a tiny but lucrative sector. Those who completed identical degrees in (say) 2000 were not so fortunate, as all-too-many of them know. Likewise, who predicted that the *public sector* would prosper under President Bush? And what happened to those who then prepared for public service, under President Obama, the chief executive of the fiscal cliff and the sequester?

The changing geography of American income inequality

Next we turn to a discussion of income inequalities measured across geographic entities, including states and their subdivisions, the counties. As shown above, variation in earnings across 21 sectors exceeds variation in earnings across the 51 states. But there is, nevertheless, substantial geographic dispersion of earnings, and even more of incomes. At the state level, per capita income ranged from $27,028 in Mississippi to $57,746 in Washington D.C. in 2006; county average income spanned $9,140 per person in Loup, Nebraska, to $110,292 in New York, New York. In this section we explore these differences.

Method and measurement

The BEA definition of income includes wages and salaries, but also incorporates rent, interest and dividends, government transfer payments, and other sources.[6] As such, income provides a broader picture of economic well-being than earnings. The ideal dataset for studying income inequality would include regular measurements of income for all individuals or households along with geographical and demographic identifiers. Such data exists in the form of income tax returns, at least for those required to file, but researchers do not have access to individual records. Thus the major work on top incomes (Piketty, 2014) stratifies by percentiles, a useful procedure but one that leaves much to the imagination.

On the other hand, the BEA uses tax records to produce income estimates for each county in the United States annually.[7] Together with population records, these data are provided through Local Area Personal Income Statistics in the Regional Economics Accounts (BEA 2008). Given this annual data set, we can calculate Theil's T for between-county income inequality.[8] Income, contrary to the earnings measure, includes capital

---

[6] "Personal Income is the income that is received by all persons from all sources. It is calculated as the sum of wage and salary disbursements, supplements to wages and salaries, proprietors' income with inventory valuation and capital consumption adjustments, rental income of persons with capital consumption adjustment, personal dividend income, personal interest income, and personal current transfer receipts, less contributions for government social insurance. The personal income of an area is the income that is received by, or on behalf of, all the individuals who live in the area; therefore, the estimates of personal income are presented by the place of residence of the income recipients" (BEA 2008).

[7] Source data for BEA income estimates come from a host of government sources, including: "The state unemployment insurance programs of the Bureau of Labor Statistics, U.S. Department of Labor; the social insurance programs of the Centers for Medicare and Medicaid Services (CMS, formerly the Health Care Financing Administration), U.S. Department of Health and Human Services, and the Social Security Administration; the Federal income tax program of the Internal Revenue Service, U.S. Department of the Treasury; the veterans benefit programs of the U.S. Department of Veterans Affairs; and the military payroll systems of the U.S. Department of Defense" (BEA 2008). We have not yet updated these measures through 2012.

[8] "Counties are considered to be the "first-order subdivisions" of each State and statistically equivalent entity, regardless of their local designations (county, parish, borough, etc.). Thus, the

gains and other returns from capital assets. Our logic is the same as before. Changes in between-county income inequality have two components – changes in relative population and changes in relative incomes. Inequality declines when poor counties add income faster than rich counties or middle income counties add population faster than counties at either tail of the distribution. When rich counties get relatively richer, poor counties get relatively poorer, or middle income counties lose population share, inequality rises.

The evolution of between-county income inequality

From 1969 to 2006, between-county income inequality in the United States increased, but the path was not smooth. From 1969 to 1976 cross-county inequality declined. A steady rise in inequality occurred until the mid-1980s, and then accelerated through the end of the decade. 1990 to 1994 saw another decline, but another reversal pushed inequality to new heights through 2000. An equally steep decline followed through 2003. Figure 7 plots two series of U.S. income inequality, the Census Bureau between-household measure and our own between-county measure.

Since the early 1970s, the two series show similar trends, a sharp rise in income inequality during the 1980s and a peak and trough around the information technology boom and bust. Between-county inequality shows greater relative variability during this period.

---

following entities are considered to be equivalent to counties for legal and/or statistical purposes: The parishes of Louisiana; the boroughs and census areas of Alaska; the District of Columbia; the independent cities of Maryland, Missouri, Nevada, and Virginia; that part of Yellowstone National Park in Montana; and various entities in the possessions and associated areas" (National Institute of Standards and Technology 2002).

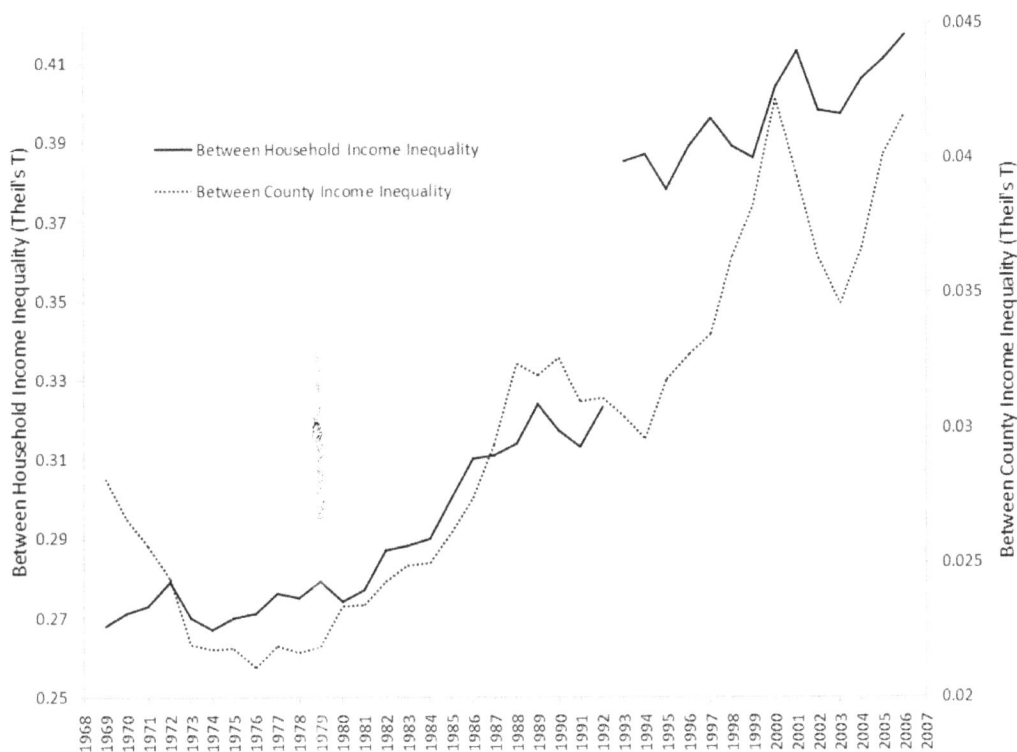

Figure 7. U.S. Income Inequality 1969–2006

The movements of between-state income inequality and between-county income inequality are closely related, but the volatility of the latter is markedly greater. Figure 8 plots the between-state component and sum of the within-state components of county income inequality from 1969 to 2006. The height of the bar represents total between-county inequality, and the white portion represents the between-state component.

Despite the close association in the annual movements of the between-state and between-county series, state per-capita incomes converged during the 1969 to 2006 period while county and household incomes grew further apart. The reduction in state income variation occurred as the South became more closely integrated with the nation as a whole over the last 40 years. For example, although still the lowest in the nation, per capita income in Mississippi has grown from 62% of national per capita income in 1969 to 74% of national per capita income in 2006. Alabama, Arkansas, Georgia, South Carolina, North Carolina, and Tennessee made similar gains.

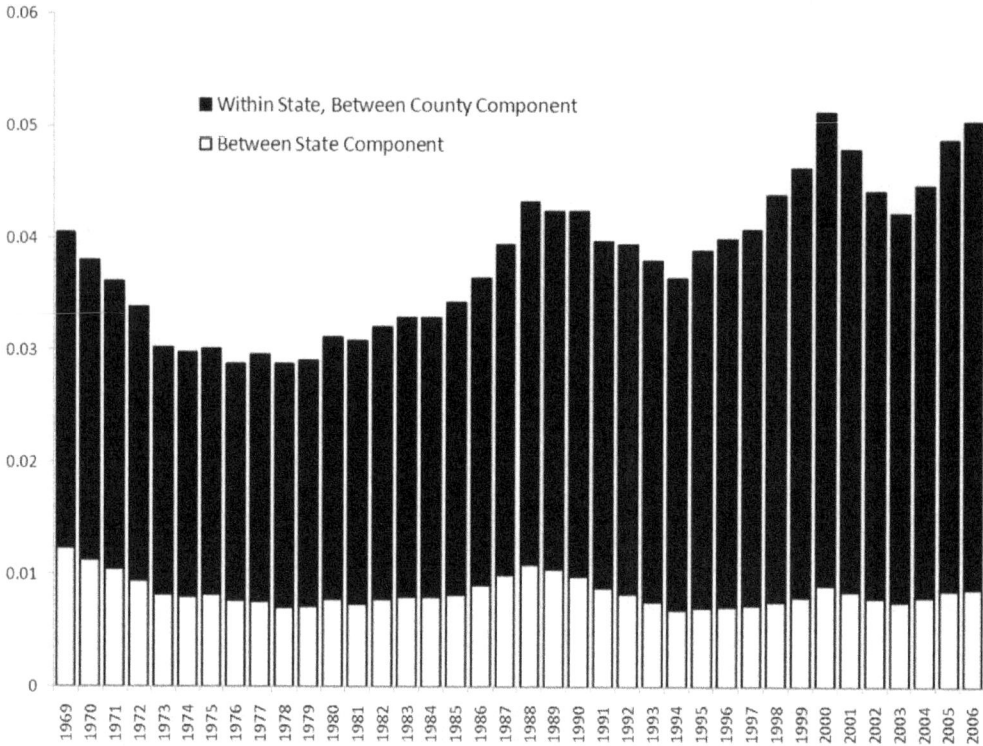

Figure 8. Components of Theil's T Statistic of Between-County U.S. Income Inequality 1969–2006

The information-technology boom, the bust, and beyond

From January 1994 to February 2000, the tech-heavy NASDAQ Composite index rose from 776.80 to 4,696.69, a 605% increase. Enthusiasts celebrated the bull market as evidence that the "new economy" would drive American prosperity into the future. Liberals (and not only liberals) lamented the spectacular rises in high-end pay and of inequality more generally. Few noted that the two phenomena were identical. Figure 9 matches the level of between-county income inequality – lagged one year – against the natural logarithm of the NASDAQ Composite. The two series move together seamlessly from 1992 to 2004, with the same peaks and troughs and the same proportional change.

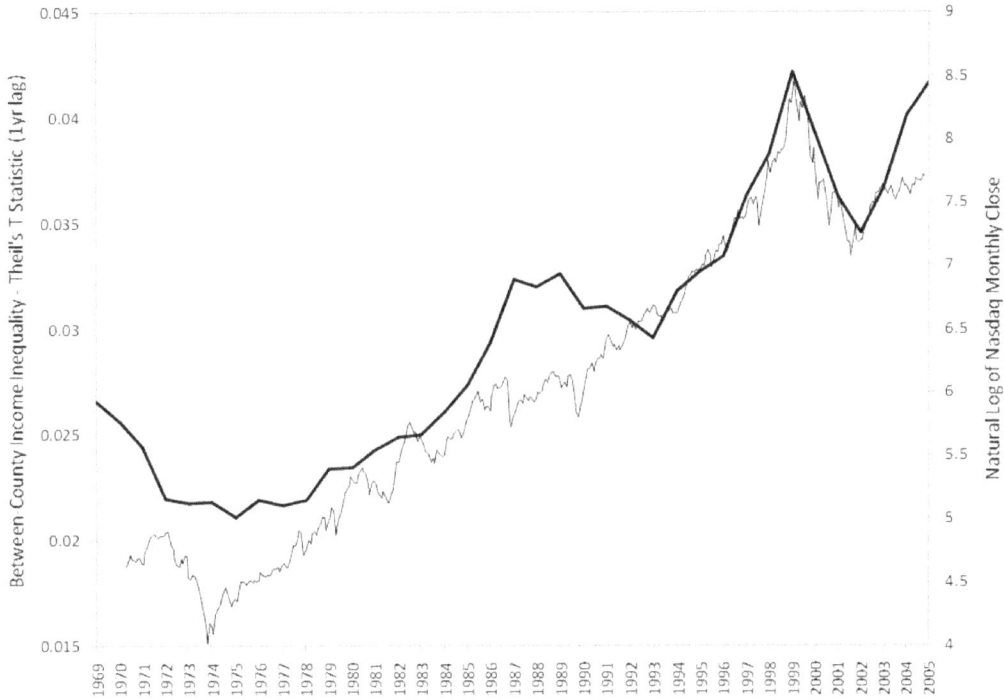

Figure 9. Theil's T Statistic of U.S. Between-County Income Inequality 1969–2006 Plotted Against the Natural Logarithm of the NASDAQ Composite Index

As technology firms' stock prices rose, their employees (especially their executives) and stockholders reaped the benefits in the form of options realizations and capital gains. If employment and share ownership in the technology sector had been uniformly distributed, this would have had little impact on the between-county measure of inequality. But technological firms were and are concentrated around such cities as San Francisco, Seattle, Raleigh, Austin, and Boston. The financiers are concentrated in Manhattan. Income growth in the counties comprising these areas accounted for almost all of the inequality increase between counties in the late 1990s, and when the information technology boom ended in 2000, falling relative incomes in these same areas reduced aggregate between-county inequality.

In particular, the four counties that contributed most to the increase in between-county income inequality from 1994 to 2000 also contributed most to the inequality decline from 2000 to 2003 – New York, NY; Santa Clara, CA; San Mateo, CA; and San Francisco, CA.

Table 3. County Population and Per Capita Income for Selected Counties 1994, 2000, 2003, 2006

Population	1994	2000	2003	2006
San Francisco, CA	742,316	777,669	759,056	756,376
San Mateo, CA	674,871	708,584	698,132	700,898
Santa Clara, CA	1,561,366	1,686,621	1,678,189	1,720,839
New York, NY	1,503,909	1,540,934	1,577,267	1,612,630
U.S.	263,125,821	282,194,308	290,447,644	298,754,819
Per Capita Income	**1994**	**2000**	**2003**	**2006**
San Francisco, CA	$ 33,164	$ 55,658	$ 53,864	$ 69,942
San Mateo, CA	$ 33,628	$ 58,893	$ 52,235	$ 66,839
Santa Clara, CA	$ 29,255	$ 54,183	$ 46,569	$ 55,735
New York, NY	$ 56,905	$ 85,752	$ 82,904	$ 110,292
U.S.	$ 22,172	$ 29,845	$ 31,504	$ 36,714

The rebound in inequality from 2003 to 2006 was of two pieces. First, many though not all, of the technology and finance counties experienced renewed income growth – New York County most of all. Second, there was a concentration of increasing income around Washington D.C., thanks to the federal government, and in Southern California, New Orleans, Las Vegas, and Southern Florida, areas central to the mortgage-finance boom.

Thus rising geographic income inequality from 1994 to 2000 was largely an artifact of the information-technology boom. That bust inflicted large, arbitrary and unnecessary losses on many who were not prepared to shoulder them. Nevertheless, as Robert Shapiro, former Under Secretary for Economic Affairs in the Department of Commerce, wrote:

"The American bubble represented an excess of something that in itself has real value for the economy – information technologies. The bubble began in overinvestment in IT and spread to much of the stock market; but at its core,
much of the IT was economically sound and efficient. Further, these dynamics also played a role in the capital spending boom of the 1990s, and much of that capital spending translated into permanently higher productivity. The result is that the American bubble should not do lasting damage to the American economy" (2002).

To this, we add that full employment achieved in the late 1990s raised living standards broadly and engendered lasting productivity gains, as well as demonstrating that full employment can be achieved without inflation, something much of the economics profession had not believed possible before that time.
From 2003 to 2006, the region around the national capital thrived. Much of this was related to the growth of military activities with wars in Afghanistan and Iraq. However federal civilian spending also grew rapidly, and there was also substantial growth in spending by private sector lobbies. Income growth in Southern California and other areas was likely related to the mortgage-finance boom, the phenomenon that led to the financial crisis.

The economic consequences should, as with the earlier period, be judged in part by the worth of the activities undertaken. However, it is already clear that the 2000s saw no very broad revival of private-sector economic dynamism. A main economic beneficiary of government spending was the government itself and those associated with it. Given the broad ideology of the incumbent administration, this is, as we've said before, ironic.

Interpreting inequality

Even before the onset of the financial crisis, economic inequality was on its way to becoming a bipartisan concern, at least so far as political rhetoric goes. Thus, President Bush:

"I know some of our citizens worry about the fact that our dynamic economy is leaving working people behind. We have an obligation to help ensure that every citizen shares in this country's future. The fact is that income inequality is real; it's been rising for more than 25 years. The reason is clear: We have an economy that increasingly rewards education, and skills because of that education... And the question is whether we respond to the income inequality we see with policies that help lift people up, or tear others down." – President Bush; State of the Economy Report Address at Federal Hall, New York; Jan. 31, 2007

A week later, Federal Reserve Chairman Ben Bernanke put it this way:

"Thus, these three principles seem to be broadly accepted in our society: that economic opportunity should be as widely distributed and as equal as possible; that economic outcomes need not be equal but should be linked to the contributions each person makes to the economy; and that people should receive some insurance against the most adverse economic outcomes, especially those arising from events largely outside the person's control." – Chairman of the Federal Reserve Ben Bernanke, Remarks before the Greater Omaha Chamber of Commerce; February 6, 2007

Perhaps most striking, in an appearance on the Charlie Rose Show on September 20, 2007, former Federal Reserve Chairman Alan Greenspan said flatly, "You cannot have a market capitalist system if there is a significant mood in the population that its rewards are unjustly distributed." Whether sincerely offered or not, these comments echo the concerns of policy makers and analysts on the Left (e.g., Neckerman 2004), who emphasize the effect of inequality on health, education, and democratic participation.

There is little doubt that when rising inequality reflects higher unemployment and lower pay at the bottom of the scale, the measure of inequality captures a major economic problem. But inequality in earnings and incomes can rise in response to growing employment, or innovation or speculation – under circumstances where no one is actually losing ground. In such cases it is necessary to take a more subtle view. Consider the relationship between changes in employment and changes in U.S. between-county income inequality, as shown in Figure 10.

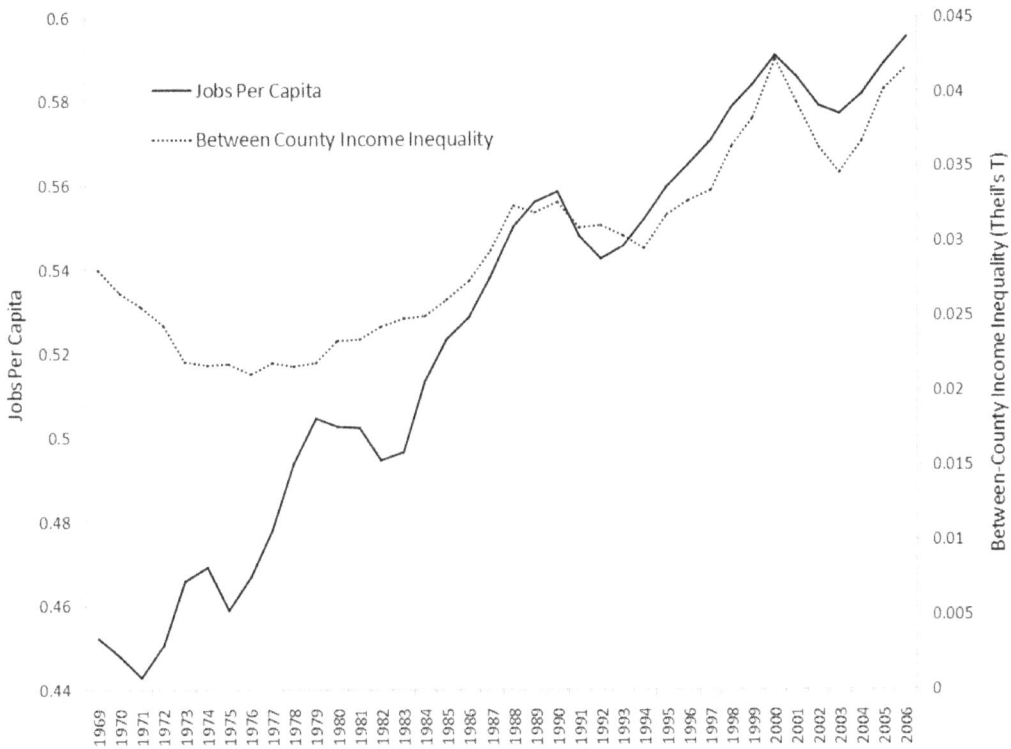

Figure 10. U.S. Between-County Income Inequality and Jobs Per Capita 1969–2006

From 1969 to 1989 the series measuring inequality and jobs-per capita are only loosely linked. Over this period, the levels have a correlation of 0.47, and year-to-year changes are almost totally uncorrelated. However, since 1990, employment and inequality have moved together. The levels have a correlation of 0.95 and the year-to-year changes have a correlation of 0.79. A rising tide may lift all boats, but recent business cycles have been more like waves, in which certain sectors and areas ride the peaks before crashing to the shore. This is a sign, surely, not of the social evil of inequality as such, but of the instability of bubble economies, for which, since 2007, we have paid a fearsome price.

Conclusion

In recent decades economic inequality increased, mainly due to extravagant gains by the already-rich. This type of inequality has consequences; most notably it affects the distribution of political power. Increasing incomes at the top of distribution may also ratchet up consumption in ways that filter down throughout society and cause behaviors that reduce social welfare (Frank 2007). Still, relative deprivation is not the same as absolute deprivation. Rather, the deeper issue with inequality of this type is instability: the rocket also falls. A problem with the trick of generating prosperity through inequality is that it cannot be repeated indefinitely, or even often.

Finally, the economic downturn after 2008 led to somewhat larger losses in the absolute earnings, wealth and incomes of the well-off than those the working poor. As such, the slump led, briefly, to a decrease in measured inequality within the United States. *Schadenfreude* aside, this was not especially good news. The debacle, after all, was a terrible debacle, irrespective of the effect on an inequality number. But it was not good news either, that inequality then recovered, alongside the stock market, while so little else did.

References

Bernanke, Ben. 2007. "Remarks before the Greater Omaha Chamber of Commerce," Omaha, Nebraska, February 6.

Bureau of Economic Analysis. 2008. "Regional Economic Accounts: State Annual Personal Income." Washington: U.S. Department of Commerce. (http://www.bea.gov/bea/regional/spi/).

Burtless, Gary. 2007. "Demographic Transformation and Economic Inequality" Mimeo.

Bush, George W. 2007. "State of the Economy Report Address," Federal Hall, New York, January 31.

Conceição, Pedro and Galbraith, James K. 2001. "Toward an Augmented Kuznets Hypothesis," in James K. Galbraith and Maureen Berner, eds., *Inequality and Industrial Change: A Global View*. Cambridge, Cambridge University Press.

Conceição, Pedro, James K. Galbraith, and Peter Bradford. 2000. "The Theil Index in Sequences of Nested and Hierarchic Grouping Structures: Implications for the Measurement of Inequality through Time, with Data Aggregated at Different Levels of Industrial Classification." *Eastern Economic Journal* 27: 61–74.

DeNavas-Walt, Carmen, Bernadette D.Proctor, and Jessica C. Smith. 2008. *U.S. Census Bureau Current Population Reports, P60-235, Income, Poverty, and Health Insurance Coverage in the United States: 2007*, U.S. Government Printing Office, Washington, DC, 2008.

Ferguson, Thomas, and James K. Galbraith, 1999. "The American Wage Structure, 1920-1946. Research in Economic History. Vol. 19, 205-257.

Frank, Robert H. 2007. *Falling Behind: How Rising Inequality Harms the Middle Class*. Berkeley, CA, University of California Press, 2007.

Galbraith, James K., 1998. *Created Unequal: The Crisis in American Pay*. New York, The Free Press.

Galbraith, James K. 2012, *Inequality and Instability: A study of the world economy just before the Great Crisis*. New York: Oxford University Press.

Goldin, Claudia and Lawrence F. Katz, 2008. The *Race Between Technology and Education*. Cambridge, Harvard University Press.

Greenspan, Alan and Charlie Rose. 2007. "A Conversation with Alan Greenspan." *The Charlie Rose Show*. PBS. WNET, Newark. September 20.

Jones, Arthur, Jr. and Daniel H. Weinberg. 2000. *U.S. Census Bureau Current Population Reports, P60-204, The Changing Shape of the Nation's Income Distribution*, U.S. Government Printing Office, Washington, DC, 2000.

Kuznets, Simon. 1955. "Economic growth and income inequality," *American Economic Review*, 45(1): 1-28.

McCarty, Nolan, Keith T. Poole, and Howard Rosenthal. 2006. *Polarized America*: *The Dance of Ideology and Unequal Riches*. Cambridge, MA: The MIT Press.

National Institute of Standards and Technology. 2002. "Counties and Equivalent Entities of the United States, Its Possessions, and Associated Areas." Washington: U.S. Department of Commerce. (http://www.itl.nist.gov/fipspubs/fip6-4.htm).

Neckerman, Kathryn, ed. 2004. *Social Inequality*. New York: Russell Sage Foundation.

Paulson, Henry. 2006. "Remarks at Columbia University," New York, August 1.

Piketty, Thomas, Capital in the 21st Century, Harvard University Press, 2014

Shapiro, Robert J.: "The American Economy Following the Information-Technology Bubble and Terrorist Attacks", *Fujitsu Research Institute Economic Review*, No. 6(1), 2002.

United for a Fair Economy. 2007. "CEO Pay Charts." Boston, United for a Fair Economy. http://www.faireconomy.org/research/CEO_Pay_charts.html

Appendix: NAICS Sectors

Farming	Clothing and clothing accessories stores
Forestry, fishing, related activities, and other	Sporting goods, hobby, book and music stores
Forestry and logging	General merchandise stores
Fishing, hunting, and trapping	Miscellaneous store retailers
Agriculture and forestry support activities	Nonstore retailers
Other	**Transportation and warehousing**
Mining	Air transportation
Oil and gas extraction	Rail transportation
Mining (except oil and gas)	Water transportation
Support activities for mining	Truck transportation
Utilities	Transit and ground passenger transportation
Construction	Pipeline transportation

Construction of buildings	Scenic and sightseeing transportation
Heavy and civil engineering construction	Support activities for transportation
Specialty trade contractors **Manufacturing**	Couriers and messengers
Wood product manufacturing	Warehousing and storage
Nonmetallic mineral product manufacturing	**Information**
Primary metal manufacturing	**Publishing industries, except Internet**
Fabricated metal product manufacturing	Motion picture and sound recording industries
Machinery manufacturing	Broadcasting, except Internet
Leather and allied product manufacturing	Internet publishing and broadcasting
Paper manufacturing	Telecommunications
Printing and related support activities	ISPs, search portals, and data processing
Petroleum and coal products manufacturing	Other information services
Chemical manufacturing	Insurance carriers and related activities
Plastics and rubber products manufacturing	Funds, trusts, and other financial vehicles
Wholesale trade Retail trade	**Finance and insurance**
Motor vehicle and parts dealers	Monetary authorities - central bank
Furniture and home furnishings stores	Credit intermediation and related activities
Electronics and appliance stores	Securities, commodity contracts, investments
Building material and garden supply stores	**Real estate and rental and leasing**
Food and beverage stores	Real estate
Health and personal care stores	Rental and leasing services
Gasoline stations	Lessors of nonfinancial intangible assets

Professional and technical services	**Accommodation and food services**
Management of companies and enterprises	Accommodation
Administrative and waste services	Food services and drinking places
Administrative and support services	**Other services, except public administration**
Waste management and remediation services	Repair and maintenance
Educational services	Personal and laundry services
Health care and social assistance	Membership associations and organizations
Ambulatory health care services	Private households
Hospitals	**Government and government enterprises**
Nursing and residential care facilities	Federal, civilian
Social assistance	Military
Arts, entertainment, and recreation	State government
Performing arts and spectator sports	Local government
Museums, historical sites, zoos, and parks	
Amusement, gambling, and recreation	

Adverse Childhood Experiences, Poverty, and Inequality: Toward an Understanding of the Connections and the Cures

John F. Tomer[1]
Manhattan College, New York, USA

Abstract

Despite Alfred Marshall's early recognition of the importance of mothering, human capital theory scarcely reflects the role of the home environment as a factor influencing the production of human capital. This paper looks deeply into the earliest phase of child development to understand its implications for human capital theory. Recently, important noneconomic research has revealed the growth of adverse childhood experiences (ACEs) among young children and how this impairs their brain functioning. Accordingly, this paper explores the role of ACEs for understanding the growth of poverty and inequality.

In contrast to other socio-economic theories explaining the growth of inequality of academic achievement, this paper focuses on the magnitude and growth of ACEs and poor parenting within the lower socio-economic class. Other theories no doubt have some validity, but if they leave out ACEs, they are missing a crucial causal factor. The implications of this theory for remedies to ACEs are explored. These remedies involve different ways to build human capital during the early childhood so that children will arrive at school with their brains unimpaired. The caring work of making human capital investments works better if they are part of a caring economy and part of a sensible human capital strategy.

Key Words: Adverse childhood experiences, human capital, noncognitive human capital, neuro development, educational inequality, early childhood development

1. Introduction

In 1890, Alfred Marshall wrote: "The most valuable of all capital is that invested in human beings; and of that capital the most precious part is the result of the care and influence of the mother" (as quoted in Cunha and Heckman 2009, p. 321). Despite Marshall's early recognition of the importance of mothering, modern day human capital theory scarcely

---

[1] John Tomer is Emeritus Professor of Economics at Manhattan College, Riverdale, NY 10471. The author has no personal or professional links that could bias his treatment of his subject. The author is very grateful to Betty Devine for her comments on an earlier version of this paper. This paper has not been previously published, is not currently under review at another journal, and will not be submitted to another journal.

reflects the role of parents and the home environment as factors influencing the production of human capital. Also, there has until recently been relatively limited understanding of what schooling actually does. "In the traditional investment model, schooling itself is often treated as a black box: individuals enter, something happens, and productivity ... increases" (Oreopoulos and Salvanes 2011, p. 159). The purpose of this paper is to look more deeply into the earliest phase of child development, from birth to two or three years of age, in order to understand the implications of this development for human capital theory. Recently, important noneconomic research has revealed the growing prevalence of adverse childhood experiences (ACEs) among young children and the role this plays in impairing their brain functioning and contributing to later age physical and mental ailments. Accordingly, this paper explores the role of ACEs for understanding poverty and the growth of inequality of both income and academic achievement. In doing this, the paper, of course, reviews the important contributions of James Heckman and his colleagues. Further, this paper attempts to build on Heckman's contributions and to add new human capital understandings related to ACEs and early childhood development. Finally, the paper develops some implications of these understandings for remedies for ACEs.

2. Economics, human development and the human brain

The limitations of human capital theory

Economics no doubt has been greatly enriched by the development of human capital theory. Unfortunately, however, this theory has been built upon a limited conception of human development. For the most part, human capital theory has emphasized human cognitive development and human acquisition of knowledge and skills that enable enhanced productivity and earnings. Further, human capital research has emphasized human capital formation taking place in schools in children five years old and older and in workplaces. In light of recent research findings, particularly that concerning brain development, it is becoming apparent that economics' human capital theory has a far too limited conception of human development, especially with regard to its relative neglect of noncognitive development and the brain development that takes place in early childhood. Further, human capital theory needs to incorporate the kinds of insights and theory concerning intangible capital which are developed in my earlier research (Tomer 2008).

The importance of early childhood development

Human brain development in early childhood

In contrast to the relatively even growth of one's physical body until about age 20, one's physical brain growth is most rapid from its time in utero until age four. At four years old, the human brain is ninety percent of adult size (Perry and Szalavitz 2006, p. 247). Despite this early rapid physical growth, the brain's growth at age four is far from finished; a great deal of brain development and organization takes place during later childhood and adolescence as the brain's systems become more complex and major cortical restructuring occurs. But the early childhood period is extremely important for neurodevelopment because it is a period when the brain is very sensitive to experience. Thus, it is a time of great malleability and vulnerability (Perry 2002, p. 82). Favorable development at this time makes possible the later realization of many human potentials. If, however, the young child experiences severe neglect and trauma, this can have a destructive effect and may close off the development of important later potentials.

The human brain develops sequentially starting with the brain stem, followed by the midbrain, then the limbic system, and then the cortex. This implies a hierarchical ordering from lower to higher brain regions. Each area of the brain specializes in different functions. The brainstem deals with the relatively automatic functioning related to, for example, body temperature, heart rate, and blood pressure. The midbrain deals with bodily functions which we have some control over such as appetite and sleep. The limbic system deals with emotional reactivity, sexual behavior, and attachment. The cortex deals with abstract thought, concrete thought, executive functions, and affiliation, among other things (Karr-Morse and Wiley 2012, p. 98; Perry and Szalavitz 2006, p. 248). "In order to develop properly, each area requires appropriately timed, patterned, repetitive experiences" (p. 248). This means there are time periods (*sensitive periods*) when experience can easily modify the biochemistry and architecture of neural circuits in particular parts of the brain. There are also *critical periods*, limited time periods when certain crucial kinds of brain development can only occur (Cunha and Heckman 2009, p. 331; see also Perry 2002, p. 87). Optimal development of the higher, more complex brain functioning requires healthy development experience in the lower, less complex brain systems in the right amounts and in the right sequence.

Parenting and the external environment

Why do some children grow up to be productive, responsible, kind people, and others become unproductive and abusive? An important part of the answer relates to the kind of early parenting that some children receive. Children need consistent, physical affection and need patterned, repetitive stimulation "to properly build the systems in the brain that connect reward, pleasure and human-to-human interactions" (Perry and Szalavitz 2006, p. 86). To realize their brain development potential, young children's brains need both quality and quantity of use and stimulation (Karr-Morse and Wiley 2012, p. 98). "It takes a modulated adult to monitor and balance newborn over- or under- arousal and help regulate ... [their] raw and reactive systems" (p. 100). Sometimes this requires swaddling and soothing; at other times it requires lively stimuli. In addition to being safe, nurturing, predictable, repetitive and gradual, it is important for parental care to be attuned to the child's developmental stage (Perry and Pollard 1998, p. 37). Crucial to early childhood development is the forging of a strong attachment relationship between the child and the parent(s). The attachment relationship is something that develops over time in the presence of a committed, loving caregiver (Karr-Morse and Wiley 2012, p. 193; Perry and Szalavitz 2006, pp. 85-86). In addition to providing a safe, stabile base, parents need to allow the child to explore his or her world, and thereby, develop resilience which enables them to do well in the face of external stressful situations (Perry and Pollard 1998, p. 40).

Stress and trauma

A child is subject to stress when he or she is exposed to dramatic, rapid, unpredictable changes to his or her environment which are likely to be upsetting and which may make returning to homeostasis difficult (Perry and Pollard 1998, p. 35). Trauma occurs when the stressful event is severe enough to disrupt the physical and emotional balance and security provided by the child's primary caregiver (Karr-Morse Wiley 2012, p. 103). Trauma is overwhelming stress; it is in excess of what the child can manage or bear (p. 24). Instead of inducing a fight or flight response, trauma is typically followed by freezing or dissociation (p. 25). The traumatized child is unable to restore his or her previous equilibrium. The new equilibrium is generally less favorable, less flexible, consumes more energy, and is maladaptive (Perry and Pollard 1998, p. 36).

If, instead of attuned, loving parenting, the caregiving is inconsistent, inattentive, chaotic, ignorant, abusive, or neglectful, this can be a source of stress or trauma that may adversely affect the child's brain development. Such adverse brain development has been documented through the use of advanced neuroimaging techniques (Perry 2002, p.

93). These techniques, for example, have shown dramatically different brain images for normal children compared to the brains of children experiencing extreme sensory neglect. Poor, neglectful childcare, which is experienced early and chronically, is the cause of dysregulation of the child's hypothalamic-pituitary-adrenal (HPA) axis (Karr-Morse Wiley 2012, p. 236). Such disregulation is associated with exaggerated reactivity, overly sensitive, maladaptive emotional, behavioral, and cognitive problems (sensitization) (Perry and Pollard 1998, p. 42). A child who is constantly being overstimulated by internal or external reminders of unhappy events will find it extremely difficult to pay attention to classroom learning (Karr-Morse and Wiley, pp. 37-38). "For these youth, ... delayed gratification is almost impossible. They are quite literally unable to consider the potential consequences of their behavior" (Perry and Szalavitz 2006, p. 250). Also these children tend to function at their most primitive level of self-interest (Karr-Morse and Wiley 2012, pp. 247-248). A calm, untraumatized child processes information quite differently than such a traumatized, sensitized child. "The calmer child can more readily focus on words of the teacher and, using her neocortex, engage in abstract thought and reasoning" (Perry and Szalavitz 2006, 249).

Adverse childhood experiences

In the early 1990s, Robert Anda and Vincent Felitti with the aid of the Kaiser Health Plan and the Centers for Disease Control pioneered a large empirical study of the relationship of adults' adverse childhood experiences (ACE) to these adults' physical and mental health and behaviors. The ACE studies focused on the ACE Score, "the number of 'yes' responses to questions about each of ten ACE categories (not incidents) that include: emotional, physical, and sexual abuse, emotional and physical neglect, witnessing domestic violence, growing up with mentally ill or substance abusing household members, loss of a parent, or having a household member incarcerated" (Larkin et al 2012, p. 264). Findings from the ACE studies demonstrate strong relationships between these adults' ACE scores and many health and social problems throughout their lives. In general, the research found that "ACEs are common, highly interrelated, and exert a powerful cumulative impact on human development" (p. 264). The findings support the view that "childhood stressors, such as abuse, affect the structure and function of the brain" (p. 265). The studies also show that ACEs are related to prevalent diseases (heart disease, cancer, lung disease...), health risk factors (smoking, alcohol abuse, promiscuity...), mental health (depressive disorders, anxiety, hallucinations...), and general health and social problems (p. 265; Anda et al 2006).

The link between childhood trauma, as indicated by one's ACE score, and adult outcomes is striking. "People with an ACE score of 4 were seven times more likely to be alcoholics as adults than people with an ACE score of 0. They were six times more likely to have had sex before age 15, twice as likely to be diagnosed with cancer, four times as likely to suffer emphysema. People with an ACE score above 6 were 30 times more likely to have attempted suicide" (Brooks, *NY Times* 2012). As part of their ACE research, Felitti and Anda examined the "relationship of childhood abuse and household dysfunction to many causes of death in adults" (Felitti et al 1998). They found a graded or linear relationship between the number of ACEs and each of the adult risk behaviors and diseases studied. Persons who had 4 or more ACEs, compared with those with none, had 4 to 12 fold higher risk of alcoholism, drug abuse, depression, and suicide attempts (p. 245). A study by Dube et al (2003) examined the relationship of ACEs to 6 health problems among 4 successive birth cohorts dating back to 1900. Again, the results indicated a consistent, strong, graded relationship, a long-lasting one, between adults' ACE scores and their health problems (p. 268). They found these results to be "consistent with emerging information about the neurobiological effects of early traumatic experiences on the developing brain of infants and young children" (p. 274).

The pyramid in Figure 1 below summarizes the essence of the findings from the ACE research studies.[2] The occurrence of ACEs lead to disrupted neurodevelopment, which leads to social, emotional and cognitive impairment, leading to the adoption of health-risk behaviors, further leading to adult disease, disability and social problems, all of which lead to early death.

---

[2] The initial version of this figure appeared in Felitti et al (1998, p. 256). The current revised version was obtained from workshop handouts (April 2013) prepared by Heather Larkin of the School of Social Welfare, State University of New York, Albany.

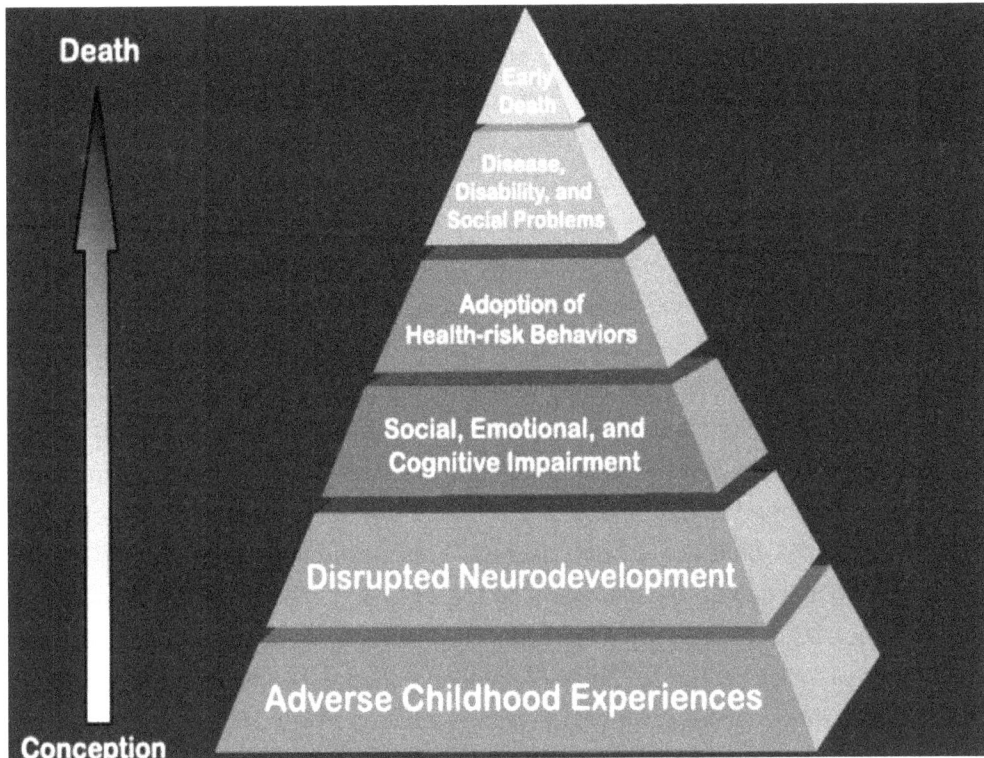

Figure 1: Influences of Adverse Childhood Experiences Throughout the Lifespan
Source: Heather Larkin's Powerpoint Presentation, March 27, 2013

3. Implications for human capital theory

James Heckman's contributions

James Heckman and his coauthors have over the last 15 years or so done much research related to early childhood human capital formation. There is no doubt that Heckman is the clear leader in this area. These research efforts have led to numerous new important insights, many of which are at odds with mainstream human capital theory. The following is a short list of important insights deriving from this research:

1. The human brain capacities developed in early childhood are crucial for the subsequent successful development of other brain capacities in later childhood

and adulthood (Heckman 2007, p. 13253; Heckman 2008, pp. 311-312; Heckman 2004, p. 197; Knudsen et al 2006, pp. 10155, 10156, 10158).

2. These crucial human brain capacities require development during certain sensitive or critical periods of early childhood (Heckman 2006, p. 1900; Knudsen et al 2006, pp. 10155, 10158, 10160).

3. The human capacities developed during early childhood are largely noncognitive ones such as self-regulation, self-control, motivation, low rates of time preference, far-sightedness, conscientiousness, adventurousness, perseverance, and tenacity that reflect the organization and regulation of the brain occurring during this time (Heckman 2007, pp. 13250, 13252).

4. The family is the major producer of human capacity in early childhood. A major factor that explains the variation among persons in human capital formation in early childhood is the quality of the child's home or family environment, which reflects the behavior of the parents. Successful family functioning in early childhood enables development of the child's human capacity, capacity that cannot be duplicated by later schooling. Adverse family environments lead to serious deficits in human capital formation during early childhood. These deficits reflect abnormal development of children's brains which can be detected by brain imaging technology (Heckman 2007, p. 13251; Heckman and Masterov 2007, pp. 447-448, 487; Heckman 2008, pp. 290, 314; Heckman 2006, pp. 1900-1901; Heckman 2004, p. 180; Knudsen et al 2006, p. 10161).

5. Adverse family environments are typically characterized by the absence of a father, low financial resources, low parental education, poor parenting skills, lack of cognitive and emotional stimulation, among other things (Heckman 2007, p. 13251; Heckman and Masterov 2007, p. 448; Heckman 2008, pp. 304-305).

6. In recent years, relatively more children are being raised in adverse environments (Heckman and Masterov 2007, p. 487; Heckman 2008, pp. 289-290, 301-302, 306; Knudsen et al 2006, p. 10155).

7. There is evidence that the rate of return on investment in human capital in early childhood is much greater than the rate of return on investment in human capital during later childhood and adulthood. Making early childhood investments in disadvantaged children is not only the fair thing to do but the societal rate of return to early childhood investment in disadvantaged children is relatively high. So it makes sense from a productivity standpoint (Heckman 2007, p. 13252;

Heckman 2008, p. 311; Heckman 2006, pp. 1901-1902; Knudsen et al 2006, p. 10161).

8. The big issue raised by these insights is: What should society do to deal with the presence and growth of adverse family environments that are leading too many people to enter adulthood with low human capital endowments? (Heckman and Masterov 2007, p. 448).

Further human capital implications

As far as I have been able to discern, Heckman does not mention the research on adverse childhood experiences. He does consider adverse family environments, poor parenting, and some of their detrimental effects, but he does not consider, at least not explicitly, ACEs, the trauma they cause, and how they severely affect the young brain. As a result, his conception of the importance of early childhood development is missing a major factor. Including ACEs in the analysis would, if anything, strengthen his analysis and policy recommendations. Moreover, the parental role in human capital formation needs more emphasis and elaboration. Accordingly, it is important to appreciate that parents not only need to prevent ACEs and other highly stressful events from impacting their children, but, to allow their child to reach his or her full potential, they need to be a nurturing, committed, attuned, consistent, loving caregivers. This parental role is extremely important, particularly in the first three years of the child's life. If things do not go well then, it will undoubtedly compromise later developmental possibilities.

Authors such as Bruce Perry and Robin Karr-Morse who are both therapists and students of brain functioning, realize that the very early years are the ones in which the child's brain is becoming organized and regulated. If this process goes poorly, the child may enter school behaving badly due to exaggerated reactivity and sensitivity, and thus, they may not be able to have a good balance of cognitive and noncognitive behavior and learning, the kind that allows them to have a satisfactory schooling experience, and which provides the basis for their next learning stage and ultimately their worklife. Without appreciation of the importance of the early years for developing balanced brain capabilities, recommendations for human capital policy are likely to be inefficient. That is, they are likely to ignore the importance of early childhood and devote too much investment to human capital formation in the later childhood years, particularly to cognitive human capital formation, in a mistaken hope that later schooling can make up for the missing brain development and noncognitive human capital formation during the early years.[3]

Children who chronically behave badly because their brain development went poorly in early childhood can be said to lack the kind of personal capital associated with emotional intelligence (see Tomer 2008, Chapter 6). Because their brains failed to develop in a healthy way, these children typically lack the ability to manage or regulate their own emotions and the ability to manage their relationships with others. In other words, such children lack emotional intelligence, a variety of personal and social competencies which are critical to educational and work achievement, and thus these children can be said to have a low personal capital endowment.

Current trends in inequality

Careful observers of trends in socio-economic inequality such as Charles Murray (2012) and Brink Lindsey (2013) have recently discerned a distinct polarization among classes. In Murray's examination of this issue, he focuses on the trends among white people since the early 1960s and finds it useful to compare the upper-middle class (top 20 percent) with the new lower class (bottom 30 percent). On many dimensions, he finds that the upper-middle class is doing relatively well; whereas the new lower class is clearly in decline. The data show polarization in the labor market as well as cultural polarization between these two classes. For example, with respect to the personal quality of industriousness, the data show that from 1970 to 2010, the percent of prime age males not in the labor force grew substantially for the bottom 30 percent relative to the top 20 percent group (Murray 2012, p. 173). Over a similar time period, for the bottom 30 percent, the percent of males with jobs who worked fewer than 40 hours in the preceding week grew significantly relative to the top 20 percent class (p. 176). And for the bottom 30 percent, the male unemployment rate compared to the national unemployment rate grew very substantially relative to the top 20 percent group (p. 175). Thus, for a variety of

---

[3] Tomer generally uses the term personal capital to refer to the developed personal qualities that reflect important aspects of an individual's functioning. Heckman, on the other hand, seems to prefer the term, noncognitive human capital. "The difference between the two is that Heckman's category is largely defined by what it is not, that is, it is not cognitive. Whereas personal capital, although largely noncognitive is defined in a more positive way, that is, personal capital is defined in terms of the specific human qualities or categories of qualities that it contains" (Tomer 2008, pp. 20-21).

reasons, males in the bottom 30 percent class had a substantially worse labor market experience than the top 20 percent which in part reflects, Murray argues, the declining industriousness of the lower middle class.

The data also supports the view that the marriage experience of the new lower class is worsening, especially relative to the upper-middle class. In 2010 the percent of whites ages 30-49 who were married among the lower 30 percent was about 50 percent compared to about 85 percent for the top 20 percent (Murray 2012, p. 154). In 1960 the respective figures were 86 and 96 percent. With regard to the percent divorced or separated, the rate for the new lower class has dramatically increased to about 35 percent, while the rate for the upper-middle class has been flat at around 7 percent for the last 30 years (p. 156). There is also a large and growing gap between these two groups in the percent of self-reported "very happy" marriages. Moreover, from a marital standpoint, the divide between the children of the bottom 30 percent and the children of the top 20 percent is large and growing. The percent of children living with a single, divorced, or separated parent for the bottom 30 percent has reached over 20 percent; whereas for the top 20 percent, it is a little over 2 percent (p. 159). Also notable is the large and rising gap between the percent of nonmarital births among mothers with 12 years or less education and mothers with a college education (p. 161). Among the new lower class, all too often, the men are not making a living and single women are raising the children. In addition, Murray has made similar comparisons illustrating the absolute and relative decline of the new lower class in regard to the qualities of honesty (including crime) and religiosity.

Reflecting the cultural differences between the two classes, childrearing practices are sharply different between the two groups.

> "The children of the new upper class[4] are the object of intense planning from the moment the woman learns she is pregnant. She sets about researching her choice of obstetrician immediately (if she hasn't already done it in anticipation of the pregnancy), and her requirements are stringent. She does not drink alcohol or allow herself to be exposed even to secondhand smoke during her pregnancy. She makes sure her nutritional intake exactly mirrors the optimal diet and takes classes (along with her husband) to prepare for a natural childbirth—a C-section is a last

---

[4] The new upper class is the upper segment of the upper-middle class.

resort. She gains no more and no less than the prescribed weight during her pregnancy. She breast-feeds her newborn, usually to the complete exclusion of formula, and tracks the infant's growth with the appropriate length and weight charts continually. The infant is bombarded with intellectual stimulation from the moment of birth, and sometimes from the moment that it is known that conception has occurred. The mobile over the infant's crib and the toys with which he is provided are designed to induce every possible bit of neural growth within the child's cerebral cortex" (Murray 2012, p. 39).

On the other hand:

"Mainstream America is a lot more relaxed than the new upper class about their children. I don't mean that other American parents care less, but that, as a group they are less inclined than upper-class parents to obsess about how smart their baby is, how to make the baby smarter, where the baby should go to preschool, and where the baby should go to law school. They buy the car seat that's on sale at Walmart instead of spending hours searching the web for the seat with the best test results in simulated head-on collisions. When their children get into trouble at school, they are less determined than upper-class parents to come up with reasons why it's the teacher's fault, not their child's" (Murray 2012, p.41).

The sociologist Annette Lareau in her 2003 book *Unequal Childhoods:*

"has identified a clear, class-based difference in parenting styles. Among the poor and working-class families she observed and studied, the focus of parenting was on what she calls 'the accomplishment of natural growth.' In these families, 'parents viewed children's development as unfolding spontaneously, as long as they were provided with comfort, food, shelter, and other basic support.' By contrast, for middle-class families with college-educated parents, the aim is 'concerted cultivation.' 'In these families,' Lareau writes, 'parents actively fostered and assessed their children's talents, opinions, and skills. They scheduled their children for activities. They reasoned with them.... *They made a deliberate and sustained effort to stimulate children's development and to cultivate their cognitive and social skills"* (Lindsey 2013, p. 65).

Toward a new behavioral economic model explaining inequality

One important part of the educational gap between the children of the upper-middle class and those of the new lower class is the more intensive parenting styles of the upper group. "High-income families are increasingly focusing their resources—their money, time and knowledge of what it takes to be successful in school—on their children's ... educational success" (Reardon, *NY Times* April 27, 2013). They are definitely spending more time on child care (Lindsey 2013, p. 64). And it is paying off.

> "Students growing up in richer families have better grades and higher standardized test scores, on average, than poorer students; they also have higher rates of participation in extracurricular activities and school leadership positions, higher graduation rates and higher rates of college enrollment and completion" (Reardon, *NY Times* April 27, 2013).

Much of the widening gap is because the children of the upper and upper-middle groups are increasingly entering kindergarten better prepared than the middle or lower class kids, and the gap persists throughout their schooling. This indicates the central importance of early childhood experience.

The other important part of the educational gap relates to the family environments of the new lower class. As indicated earlier, family break up has become increasingly common in this lower group as indicated especially by the growth in the percent divorced or separated and the growth in the percent of children living wth a single parent, usually the mother. Such single-parent families are not well off. "The median family income for single mothers—who are more likely to be younger, black or Hispanic, and less educated—is $23,000 (Rampell, *NY Times* May 29, 2013). Never-married mothers (whose numbers in the new lower class have grown dramatically) have even lower incomes than those who are divorced or widowed. According to economist David Autor, research shows that lower-income children raised by their mothers are at a particular disadvantage; this is especially true for their sons who on the average are believed to get fewer hours of attention from their mothers than their daughters do (Appelbaum, *NY*

Times March 20, 2013). Single mothers who generally have to work are often stressed and generally do not have a great deal of time or money to devote to child care, much less trying to give their children the special advantages that upper class children receive. In light of the above, one suspects that adverse childhood experiences are more prevalent in families headed by single parents. However, at present there is no data directly bearing on this latter issue.

The educational success gap between high- and lower- income students has grown substantially because of what upper class parents are increasingly doing and what lower class parents are increasingly unable or neglecting to do. Of course, higher income families have the monetary resources necessary to purchase the best preschool and childcare not to mention a variety of child enrichment resources and activities. Lower income families, on the other hand, are clearly constrained by the rising costs of education and childcare as well as poor job markets. This means that the children of the new lower class are arriving at kindergarten much less prepared than the children of the more affluent group. And schools, although they have tried, have not reduced this inequality (Reardon, *NY Times* April 27, 2013). Nor is there any convincing evidence that schools have increased the inequality. Thus, there has been much more, and more successful, human capital investment going on among the higher income families, particularly during early childhood. Lower class males, in particular, are apparently not responding to the rising returns to investment in human capital, especially the rising return to college education (Lindsey 2013, pp. 60-61); Appelbaum, *NY Times*, March 20, 2013). This is hard to understand. However, the analysis here points to two major causal factors. One is that elite culture is very much fostering educational achievement, while lower class culture is moving in the opposite direction (Lindsey 2013, p. 61). Second is the growing family breakup and dysfunction, which there is reason to believe is increasing the prevalence of adverse childhood experiences among the lower class. Unfortunately, data necessary to verify this supposition is not currently available. If ACEs are higher among the lower class, this will no doubt contribute to their children's educational disadvantages, and these disadvantages are not easily remedied.

Behavioral Economic Macro Model
Explaining Educational (& Income) Inequality

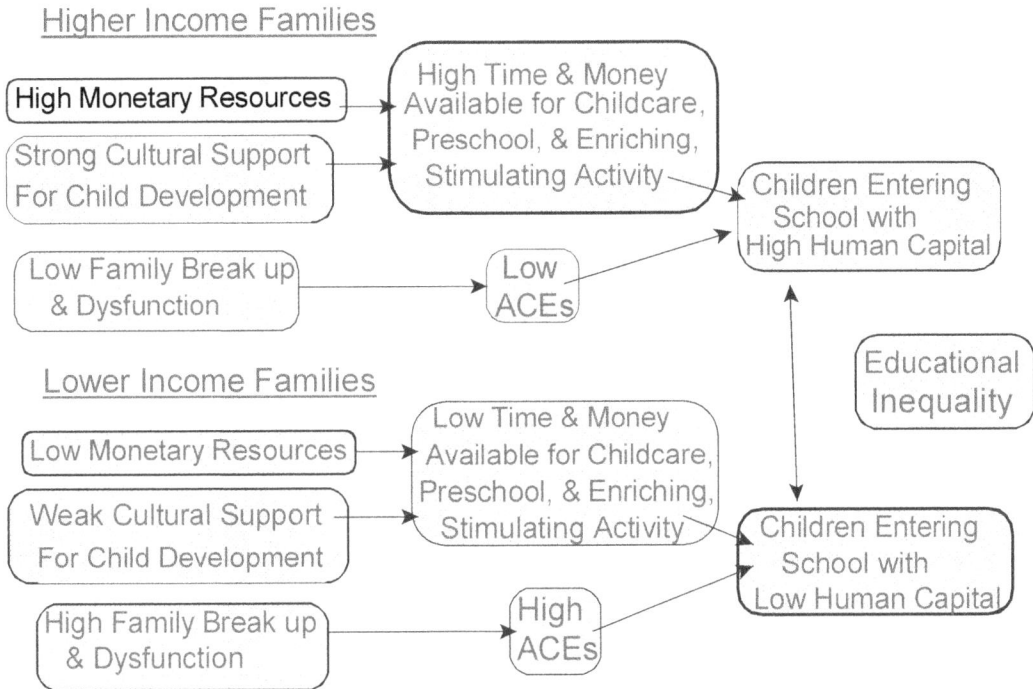

Figure 2

The explanations above constitute in essence a new behavioral economic macro model explaining educational (and income) inequality. The core features of this model are as follows and are displayed in Figure 2. For higher income families, high monetary resources and strong cultural support for child development lead to high time and money available for childcare, preschool, and enriching, stimulating activity which contributes to their children entering school with high human capital. Also making the same contribution is this group's relatively lower rates of family break up and dysfunction leading to low rates of ACEs.[5] For lower income families, low monetary resources and weak cultural

---

[5] Strictly, it is hypothesized that higher income families either have relatively low rates of ACEs or that if their ACE scores are similar to lower income families, they do much more to remedy their children's resulting psychological and social deficits arising from these experiences.

support for child development lead to low time and money available for childcare, preschool, and enriching, stimulating activity which contributes to their children entering school with low human capital. Also making the same contribution is the group's relatively high rates of family break up and dysfunction leading to high rates of ACEs. The gap between the human capital endowments of children from higher income families and those of lower income families at school entry constitutes the educational inequality which presumably leads in later years to income inequality. The model offered here is intended to provide an important explanation for inequality, but not necessarily one that is at odds with other worthy explanations such as the ones cited below. It is anticipated that testing the model's main hypothesis will not be an easy task given the current lack of data on the incidence of ACEs among socio-economic classes. Note that in Figure 2, human capital refers to both cognitive and noncognitive human capital - the noncognitive human capital or personal capital arguably being the more significant part in very early childhood.

This paragraph and the next contrast briefly the main argument above concerning the cause of the growth in educational (and consequent income) inequality with competing causal explanations. First, Murray's (2012) account focuses to a great extent on character as the key causal variable. For example, in his analysis, it is the decline of industriousness, honesty, and religiosity of the new lower class that contribute to the rise in their poor behaviors and outcomes such as relatively low income and happiness. Lindsey's analysis, on the other hand, focuses largely on the cognitive ability, especially fluency with abstraction, of the relatively high income elites who invest in this type of human capital that society needs most given the growing complexity of the socio-economy. Lindsey's account gives almost no consideration to the childhood problems or adversities of the lower income groups, but he does briefly mention "the collapse of the traditional nuclear family structure among the less educated" and the "divorce divide along educational lines" as well as pointing to cultural polarization and that many lower income people are not responding to the substantial incentives to invest in needed human capital.

In their book review essay article, Acemoglu and Autor (2012) outline a more mainstream economic theory that explains the growth of income inequality among higher, middle, and lower income groups. A key factor in their analysis is the growth of factor augmenting or skill-biased technology. In recent times, this kind of technological change has arguably complemented the skills of high skill workers and has tended to substitute for the skills of middle skill workers. Thus, this technological change leads to an increased demand for high skill workers and a declining demand for middle skill workers as the latter are displaced with the installation of the new technology. In recent periods, the wage premium for high skill relative to middle skill workers has increased. This is the expected result because the supply of high skill workers (with college and post-college education) has not kept up with the demand, whereas the supply of middle skill workers has kept up, or more than kept up, with the sagging demand for them. An important implication of this theory is that there is a great need to improve the efficacy and efficiency of U.S. education at all levels but especially in order to increase the supply of high skill workers (p. 460). This mainstream theory no doubt has validity, but their account leaves no room for alternative considerations relating to noncognitive human capital and to adverse childhood experience. Thus, it fails to come to terms with important reasons for the educational gap between higher and lower income groups, which arguably are elements necessary for a full understanding of inequality and what human capital policies would be most appropriate to deal with it.

4. Toward a cure for the problem

The heart of the problem as outlined earlier is the poor parenting and adverse childhood experiences that sabotage early childhood neurodevelopment leaving children with reduced human capacities for later life learning and work. In contrast to most economists in the human capital field, Heckman and Masterov (2007) understand the essence of what needs to be done.

> "It makes sense to invest in young children from disadvantaged environments. Substantial evidence shows that these children are more likely to commit crime, have out-of-wedlock births, and drop out of school. Early interventions that partially remediate the effects of adverse environments can reverse some of the harm of disadvantage and have a high economic return. They benefit not only the children themselves, but also their children, as well as society at large" (p. 446).

Heckman and Masterov point out that postschool remediation programs such as public job training and general educational development (GED) cannot make up for the damage done in early childhood (p. 447). To successfully deal with the problem requires supplementing the childrearing resources of disadvantaged families during early childhood (p. 448). "Millions of parents don't have the means, the skill or, in some cases, the interest in building their children's future" (Brooks *NY Times*, February 14, 2013).

Therefore, these disadvantaged parents need the special kinds of help that will either enable their children to pass through early childhood with their brain development unimpaired or provide remedial help for the child's early impairment in order that they can be fully ready for later childhood development and learning.

A remedy for the worst cases

For children who have experienced severe trauma and consequent severe impairment of their neurodevelopment in their early years, the neurosequential approach developed by Bruce Perry, psychiatrist and Ph.D., is a remedy that has worked in many cases. This approach is based on the understanding that neural systems organize and become functional in a sequential manner starting from the lower and proceeding to the higher brain regions (Perry and Szalavitz 2006, pp. 138-139). In the neurosequential approach, the therapist provides the child with "patterned repetitive experiences appropriate to their developmental needs, needs that reflect the age at which they'd missed important stimuli or had been traumatized, not their chronological age" (p. 138). One example is cuddling a seven year old boy, providing the touch and rhythm he had missed as an infant (p. 138). The key is for the therapist to discover the brain regions and functions that are underdeveloped or poorly functioning and then figure out how to help the child gain the missing stimulation or developmental experience (p. 248). In treating a traumatized child, the therapist must create an atmosphere of safety and develop a predictable, respectful, nurturing relationship (p. 154). Another key part of the process is calming the child's stress response system enabling the child to rely on their higher brain functioning, thereby reducing the child's sensitization or high arousal time (p. 250).

One of Perry's significant therapeutic stories is that of Sandy, a girl who witnessed the murder of her mother, had her throat slit, and was left for dead at age 3 (Perry and Szalavitz 2006, pp. 31-56). Not surprisingly, in the nine months until her therapy with Perry began around age four, Sandy suffered from severe mental difficulties. Sandy had profound sleep problems, was pervasively anxious, and had a high startle response, jumping at the slightest unexpected noise (p. 42). Sometimes she had aggressive, tantrum-like outbursts; she was especially afraid of knives; and she had become sensitized (pp. 42-43). An important part of the therapy was for Perry to allow Sandy to reenact the traumatizing experience, thus enabling her to gain tolerance for her traumatized memories, gaining control of her life, and gradually reducing her sensitization. It was a slow process but the reenactments along with the safe, nurturing therapeutic environment were able to transform Sandy and eliminate her symptoms (p. 56). Sometime later, Perry reported that Sandy had "made friends, got good grades, and was notably kind and nurturing in her interactions … [and is] having the kind of satisfying and productive life we had all wanted for her" (p. 56). Many other interesting examples of Perry's therapeutic approach to helping children who were early childhood victims of severe neglect and trauma can be found in other chapters of Perry and Szalavitz (2006).

Perry and his colleagues' work helping children overcome their severe victimization is an excellent example of human capital investment in early childhood. But, is this a remedy that can be applied broadly? After all, Perry is an outstanding psychiatrist and innovator in this field. Would it be possible to train enough therapists with sufficient skills to successfully treat all the children in need of this service? Would it make sense to devote a very large amount of resources to this effort? From a purely economic standpoint, the answer depends on the rate of return to this investment. Another way to look at the question is to ask: can we afford the wasted lives and social discord of not making such investments? To definitively answer this question, it is also necessary to consider two broad alternatives to intensive therapy. First are approaches that would prevent early childhood neural impairment from occurring in the first place. Second is utilizing less costly approaches that provide remedies for the many children who are less severely impacted by adverse family environments.[6]

Preventative approaches

As writers in the child development field generally recognize, it is much better to prevent child maltreatment than it is to rely on remedies after it occurs (see, for example, World Health Organization 2006, p. 8). What circumstances would prevent children from experiencing the neglect and trauma that lead to impaired neurodevelopment of their brains? The consensus answer is an environment in which all children lived with both parents who provide a safe, nurturing, loving environment and who have sufficient and relatively secure income sources. Under these circumstances, it is very unlikely that their children would encounter development compromising adverse experiences. This answer suggests the kinds of prevention that are needed. First, poverty (entailing low income) or

---

[6] An alternative to the therapy Perry writes about is a treatment called child-parent psychotherapy in which parents can work with therapists to improve parent-infant attachment relationships and attempt to overcome the effects of trauma. A scientific evaluation of this type of therapy found it to be successful in a high percentage of cases (Tough 2012, p. 38).

the threat of it needs to be prevented. Second, low quality parenting needs to be prevented. Third, divorce and separation need to be prevented.

The first type of prevention can be achieved through paid parental leave (Perry and Szalavitz 2006, p. 235; Pressman and Scott forthcoming; Heckman and Masterov 2007, p. 448; Karr-Morse and Wiley 2012, p. 245). The goal of this policy is to overcome poverty in families with infants in order to counter the many negative consequences of poverty, especially for the child and mother (Pressman and Scott forthcoming, pp. 1-11). Paid parental leave can be viewed as an investment in human capital in that these governmental transfers to parents should enable the parents to provide more and better child care yielding substantial benefits. The most important of these benefits is enabling children to avoid brain impairment; this in effect raises these children's mental capacities. Unlike many economically developed European countries, the U.S. lacks a paid parental leave program. Mainly because of this, child poverty rates in the U.S. are far higher than those in other developed nations (Pressman and Scott forthcoming, p. 20).

The second type of prevention involves improving parenting. If the parental environment plays a key role in children's neurodevelopment, and if, too often, parents are failing in this role, it makes sense to invest in parents' human capital in order to improve the quality of their parenting (Reardon, *NY Times* 2013).

> "This means finding ways of helping parents become better teachers themselves. This might include strategies to support working families so that they can read to their children more often. It also means expanding programs like the Nurse-Family Partnership that have proved to be effective at helping single parents educate their children" (Reardon).

As Perry and Szalavitz (2006, p. 237) note, it is important to educate parents about the needs of infants and how to address them. Ideally, efforts along this line can help create a more infant- and child-literate society. Parents can also benefit from simply learning to take the time to pay attention and listen to their children (p. 244). Karr-Morse and Wiley (2012, p. 243) has proposed the creation of a 'Parenting Institute' which "would bring together key units of emotional developmental information from world-renowned experts, combined with the fundamentals of brain science." Note also that it is possible to improve the parental environment by including extended family members in childcare, especially the grandparents (Perry & Szalavitz 2006, p. 237).

Healthy Families New York has been particularly successful in helping new parents who are at risk for child maltreatment. Their Home Visiting Program has provided intensive in-home services to parents until their children enter school. These services are designed to promote positive parenting skills and parent-child bonding and interaction, prevent child abuse and neglect, promote child health and development, and enhance family self-sufficiency. A careful study of the child outcomes seven years later indicated the success of the program. Compared to a control group, children in the home-visited group were substantially less likely to repeat first grade, and performed above grade level in three behaviors that promote learning. Girls, especially, in this program were much more likely to perform above grade level on reading and math compared to the control group (based on a summary of details from Kirkland and Mitchell- Herzfeld (2012)).

The third type of prevention involves either preventing divorce or separation or providing a way for the missing parent, usually the father, to be available for regular parenting. If more marriages could be saved or more missing fathers could resume involvement in their children's lives, that would certainly be helpful (Appelbaum, *NY Times* 2013). It should be noted that there is no point in trying to keep husband and wife together if domestic violence is the highly likely outcome. That could be worse for the children than a marital breakup. In any case, there is a clear need for domestic violence services for victims and batterers as well as fatherhood programs which engage and teach young men how to be a father for their children. There is not sufficient space here to consider all the many things that could be done in this general vein.[7]

Remedies for moderately disadvantaged children

This section deals briefly with the kind of remedies suitable for moderately disadvantaged children, but not children requiring intensive individual therapy. The main candidate here is enriched preschool. The "flagship" example is the Perry Preschool Program. Because of its worthwhile features and because of the availability of data and analysis on it, it makes sense to focus on this program despite the fact that there are many other variants of enriched preschool.

---

[7] For a more practical and comprehensive treatment of the subject, prevention of child maltreatment, see World Health Organization (2006, pp.32-49).

The Perry Preschool started in Ypsilanti, Michigan in the mid-1960s as a two year experimental intervention for disadvantaged three and four year old African-Americans (Tough 2012, pp. xix-xxi). The children chosen were ones with relatively low IQ and socio-economic status; no children with untreatable mental defects were chosen (Heckman et al 2010, p. 116). The chosen children were randomly assigned to either a treatment group (Perry Preschool) or a control group (no preschool). The school program involved two and a half hour weekday morning sessions and a one and a half hour afternoon visit by a teacher to the child's home once a week (Heckman and Masterov 2007, p. 478; Heckman 2008, p. 308). The purpose of the latter was to involve the child's mother in the educational process:

> "the curriculum was based on supporting children's cognitive and socio-emotional development through *active learning* where both teachers and children had major roles in shaping children's learning. Children were encouraged to plan, carry out, and reflect on their own activities through a plan-do-review process" (Heckman et al 2010, p. 116).

Follow-up interviews were done when the children reached ages 15, 19, 27, and 40 years old (p. 116). Information from these interviews has enabled researchers to learn how the preschool participants were doing in later life relative to the control group.

The findings from the Perry Preschool experiment are very noteworthy. First the preschool children's test scores showed an initial IQ improvement, but this did not last after the third grade. The more important finding was the improvement in the preschool children's noncognitive skills such as curiosity, self-control, social fluidity, and motivation (Tough 2012, p. xx; Heckman 2008, p. 308). These improvements led in turn to a large number of improved behaviors and outcomes (relative to the control group). These included: more likely to graduate from high school, more likely to earn more than $25,000 at age 40, less crime and delinquency, greater literacy, higher achievement test scores, decreased grade retention, reduced time in special education, more likely employed, less likely on welfare, lower teenage pregnancy, higher marriage rates, better jobs, more likely to own home, and higher 4 year college participation rate. As Heckman and Masterov (2007, p. 487 point out, the preschool intervention's greatest impact was in creating the attitudes and motivation (noncognitive qualities) that ultimately lead to the favorable outcomes.

It is important to note that preschools cannot duplicate what a well-functioning family gives its children (Heckman and Masterov 2007, p. 487). But enriched preschool can to some extent make up for the lack of a well-functioning family. That is what the Perry Preschool apparently has done. Moreover, programs like Perry Preschool that have a home visit component can "affect the lives of the parents and create a permanent change in the home environment," a change which continues to support the child even after the preschool has ended (Heckman 2008, p. 314). Heckman and his colleagues (2010) have attempted a careful, rigorous assessment of the Perry Preschool Program using the data from the intervention and the follow-ups. They estimate that "the overall annual social rate of return to the Perry program is in the range of 7-10 percent" (p. 115). These researchers also find that "the benefit-cost ratio for the Perry program ... ranges from 7 to 12 dollars per person, i.e., each dollar invested returns in present value terms 7 to 12 dollars back to society" (pp. 115-116). In other words, from a conventional economic standpoint, the investment in the Perry Preschool was very successful.

It is worth noting that the Obama Administration's recent preschool proposal has a general similarity to the Perry Preschool Program (see, for example, Brooks, *NY Times* February 14, 2013). One important difference is that the Perry program was only targeted at disadvantaged children; whereas the Obama plan aspires to "make high-quality preschool available to every single child in America."

As explained earlier, critical brain development occurs very early in childhood, and adverse childhood experiences and poor parenting can prevent necessary neurodevelopment from occurring. For this reason, it is important for remedial childcare to occur very early when young brains are plastic. That is why the Abecedarian Program is of particular interest. This program, like the Perry Program, served disadvantaged, mostly Afro-American children. The Abecedarian program started earlier (age 4 months), was more intensive (6-8 hours per day), and lasted longer (close to five years) than the Perry Preschool (Heckman 2006, p. 1901; Heckman and Masterov 2007, pp. 479, 481, 484-486). The Abecedarian Program's relatively favorable outcomes may at least in part be due to its starting earlier in the child's life.

One other preschool intervention should be noted. The intervention during the early 1990s in Jamaica involved psychosocial stimulation and nutritional supplementation of growth-retarded toddlers living in poverty (Gertler et al 2013). "The intervention consisted of one-hour weekly visits from community Jamaican health workers over a 2-year period that taught parenting skills and encouraged mothers to interact and play with their children in ways that would develop their children's cognitive and personality skills"

(p. i). Twenty years later, the study participants were re-interviewed and the findings were analyzed carefully. The nutritional intervention did not have a long-term impact, but the stimulation "proved to have large impacts on cognitive [and psychosocial] development 20 years later" (p. 2). The analysis also showed that the stimulation increased average earnings of the participants (then about 22 years old) by 42 percent compared to the control group.

5. Needed: a caring economy and economics

According to Riane Eisler (2007; 2012), the problems associated with the lack of adequate childcare are part of a larger problem, i.e., the lack of a caring economy. And the latter is related to the fact that caring is not a central part of the economics discipline. Eisler (2007, pp. 16-17) defines caring work as "actions based on empathy, responsibility, and concern for human welfare and optimal human development." In Eisler's view, the economy's rules and practices too often fail to satisfactorily value the "most essential human work: the work of caring for ourselves, others, and our Mother Earth." One part of the difficulty is that the household sector is generally excluded from the economic map toward which our economic thinking is directed. This is significant because the household sector is an important locus of caring behavior, especially early childhood caring (pp. 12-14). The exclusion of the household sector makes it difficult for economists, much less noneconomists, to think about how the economy's caring problems can be solved and how this is related to a more general difficulty, lack of full human development. What is needed is developing a more caring economy and economics, which would enable us to attain "a future where all children have the opportunity to realize their potential for consciousness, empathy, caring, and creativity—capacities that make us fully human" (Eisler 2012, p. 82). It is a future in which the full development of human capital of all people in higher and lower classes would be emphasized. In a caring economy, the recent breakdown of the household sector among the lower socio-economic classes and the deterioration of childhood caring there would not be tolerated.

6. A human capital future

Another useful overarching perspective is provided by Thomas Courchene (2001) who envisioned a "human capital future for Canadians." In an era of globalization and the rapid spread of knowledge and information technologies, Courchene realized that Canada needed to make a transition from a resource and physical capital based economy to an economy and society that was more competitive and based on skill. Moreover, he strongly believed that competitiveness needed to be integrated or balanced with equality of opportunity and social cohesion. Thus, the key to his economic development strategy is skill (or human capital) development for all citizens. And as Courchene pointed out, "the family is the effective locus for the production of human capital" (p. 11). Therefore, in keeping with his overarching themes, it makes sense to put a strong emphasis on early childhood development in order to counter adverse childhood experiences and growing inequality, and thereby build the needed human capital.

7. Conclusions

"The most reliable way to produce an adult who is brave and curious and kind and prudent is to ensure that when he is an infant, his hypothalamic-pituitary-adrenal axis functions well. And how do you do that? It is not magic. First, as much as possible, you protect him from serious trauma and chronic stress; then, even more important, you provide him with a secure, nurturing relationship with one parent and ideally two" (Tough 2012, p. 182).

The model developed above that explains the large educational inequality between the upper and lower income classes needs much more research. In particular, there is a need for 1) more and better data on the socio-economic incidence of ACEs and 2) sound empirical analysis to test the hypothesis embodied in the model. Nevertheless, more and more children from lower income, lower socio-economic backgrounds seem to be coming from broken homes and have single parents. There is at least some reason to believe that these are the children most likely to have high ACE scores and less likely to have a secure attachment with a parent. Moreover, there is evidence that they have below-average executive function skills, difficulty handling stressful situations, poor concentration in the classroom, inability to sit still and follow directions, impaired social skills, and are perceived as misbehaving (p. 192). These children need and deserve help. They need the kind of carefully targeted human capital investment that will enable them to ultimately arrive at school and their work with their brains unimpaired.

Because too many of these kids are not ready for school and are unable to become productive, skilled workers, fewer of them are graduating from high school and fewer are entering the labor force. Not only is this producing greater inequality but it is lowering the economy's productivity. In short, it is a waste of human resources. This is a situation that cries out for intelligent investment in humans, in particular investment in early childhood development. This paper provides some guidelines regarding the main kinds of human capital investment that are needed. It also suggests that these efforts would work best if they were part of an overall effort to create a caring economy which values the development of a high level human capital strategy.

References

Acemoglu, Daron and Autor, David. 2012. "What Does Human Capital Do? A Review of Goldin and Katz's *The Race between Education and Technology*," *Journal of Economic Literature*, 50(2), June, 426-463.

Anda, Robert F. et al. 2006. "The Enduring Effects of Abuse and Related Adverse Experiences in Childhood: A Convergence of Evidence from Neurobiology and Epidemiology," *European Archives of Psychiatry and Clinical Neuroscience*, 256, 174-186.

Applebaum, Binyamin. 2013. "Study of Men's Falling Income Cites Single Parents," *New York Times*, March 20.

Brooks, David. 2012. "The Psych Approach," *New York Times*, September 27.

Brooks, David. 2013. "When Families Fail," *New York Times,* February 14.

Courchene, Thomas J. 2001. *A State of Minds: Toward a Human Capital Future for Canadians.* Montreal, Quebec: Institute for Research on Public Policy.

Cunha, Flavio and Heckman, James J. 2009. "The Economics and Psychology of Inequality and Human Development," *Journal of the European Economic Association*, 7(2-3), April-May, 320-364.

Dube, Shanta R. et al. 2003. "The Impact of Adverse Childhood Experiences on Health Problems: Evidence from Four Birth Cohorts Dating Back to 1990," *Preventive Medicine*, 37, 268-277.

Eisler, Riane. 2007. *The Real Wealth of Nations: Creating a Caring Economics.* San Francisco: Berrett-Koehler.

Eisler, Riane. 2012. "Economics as if Caring Matters," *Challenge*, 55(2), March-April, 58-86.

Felitti, Vincent J. et al. 1998. "Relationship of Childhood Abuse and Household Dysfunction to Many of the Leading Causes of Death in Adults," *American Journal of Preventive Medicine*, 14(4), 245-258.

Gertler, P., Heckman, J, Pinto, R. Zanolini, A., Vermeerch, C., Walker, S., Chang-Lopez, S., Grantham-McGregor, S. 2013. *Labor Market Returns to Early Childhood Stimulation.* Working Paper 6529, July, World Bank.

Heckman, James J. 2004. "Lessons from the Technology of Skill Formation," *Annals of the New York Academy of Sciences*, 1038, 179-200.

Heckman, James J. 2006. "Skill Formation and the Economics of Investing in Disadvantaged Children," *Science*, 312(5782), June, 1900-1902.

Heckman, James J. 2007. "The Economics, Technology, and Neuroscience of Human Capability Formation," *Proceedings of the National Academy of Sciences*, 104(33), August 14, 13250-13255.

Heckman, James J. and Masterov, Dimitriy V. 2007. "The Productivity Argument for Investing in Young Children," *Review of Agricultural Economics*, 29(3), Autumn, 446-493.

Heckman, James J. 2008. "Schools, Skills, and Synapses," *Economic Inquiry*, 46(3), July, 289-324.

Heckman, et al. 2010. "The Rate of Return to the HighScope Perry Preschool Program," *Journal of Public Economics*, 94, 114-128.

Karr-Morse, Robin and Wiley, Meredith. 2012. *Scared Sick: The Role of Childhood Trauma in Adult Disease*. New York: Basic Books.

Kirkland, K. and Mitchell-Herzfeld, S. 2012. *Evaluating the Effectiveness of Home Visiting Services in Promoting Children's Adjustment in School: Final Report to the Pew Center for the States.* Rensselaer, New York: New York State Office of Children and Family Services.

Knudsen, Eric J. et al. 2006. "Economic, Neurobiological, and Behavioral Perspectives on Building America's Future Workforce," *Proceedings of the National Academy of Sciences*, 103(27), July 5, 10155-10162.

Larkin, Heather et al. 2012. "The Health and Social Consequence of Adverse Childhood Experiences (ACE) Across the Lifespan: An Introduction to Prevention and Intervention in the Community," *Journal of Prevention and Intervention in the Community,* 40, 263-270.

Lindsey, Brink. 2013. *Human Capitalism: How Economic Growth Has Made Us Smarter*. Princeton: Princeton University Press.

Murray, Charles. 2012. *Coming Apart: The State of White America, 1960-2010*. New York: Crown Forum.

Oreopoulos, Philip and Salvanes Kjell G. 2011. "Priceless: The NonpecuniaryBenefits of Schooling," *Journal of Economic Perspectives*. 25(1), Winter, 159-184.

Perry, Bruce D. and Szalavitz, Maia. 2006. *The Boy Who Was Raised as a Dog and Other Stories from a Child Psychiatrist's Notebook*. New York: Basic Books.

Perry, Bruce D. 2002. "Childhood Experience and the Expression of Genetic Potential: What Childhood Neglect Tells Us About Nature and Nurture," *Brain and Mind*, 3(1), April, 79-100.

Perry, Bruce D. and Pollard, Ronnie. 1998. "Homoeostasis, Stress, Trauma, and Adaptation; A Neurodevelopmental View of Childhood Trauma," *Child and Adolescent Psychiatric Clinics of North America*, 7(1), January, 33-51.

Pressman, Steven and Scott, Robert H. forthcoming. "Paid Parental Leave: A Cure for Child Poverty and a Path to Sustainable Growth," in Holt, Ric and Greenwood, Daphne. Editors. *A Brighter Future*. Armonk, NY: M.E. Sharpc.

Rampell, Catherine. 2013. "The Family Breadwinner Is More Often a Woman," *New York Times*, May 29.

Reardon, Sean F. 2013. "No Rich Child Left Behind," *New York Times,* April 27.

Rich, Motoko. 2013. "In Alabama, A Model for Obama's Push to Expand Preschool," *New York Times*, February 14.

Tomer, John F. 2008. *Intangible Capital: Its Contribution to Economic Growth, Well-being and Rationality*. Northampton, MA: Edward Elgar.

Tough, Paul. 2012. *How Children Succeed: Grit, Curiosity, and the Hidden Power of Character*. New York: Houghton Mifflin Harcourt.

World Health Organization. 2006. *Preventing Child Maltreatment: A Guide to Taking Action and Generating Evidence*, World Health Organization.

Rethinking Economics: Downs with Traction

Stuart Birks[1,2]
School of Economics and Finance, Massey University, New Zealand

Abstract

Economic theory has relatively little to say about the policy making process. One exception is Anthony Downs' *An Economic Theory of Democracy* which considers possible objectives for participants in the political process, and develops propositions on the operation of a democracy. Two key assumptions were no false information and no irrationality. As he acknowledged, neither is realistic. There is extensive literature, including writing by Adam Smith on rhetoric (deliberative eloquence) in political debate, and the significance of propaganda was recognised in the 1940s. Modern approaches to political processes, agenda setting, and discourse analysis also emphasise persuasion and framing.

This paper builds on Downs' foundation by relaxing his assumptions. First, there is consideration of the nature of rhetoric, including "macro-rhetoric". The effects of rhetoric on policy debate, and the importance of "traction" on political agendas are then considered. Propositions are presented indicating, in particular: policy issues will only be addressed spasmodically; few options will get attention; and there is likely to be poor monitoring. Consideration is then given to implications for economists and their approaches to policy.

Keywords: Rhetoric, macro-rhetoric, agenda setting, framing, traction, politics, Downs, democracy

1. Introduction[3]

Those trained in economics have come to form a view of the world that has been shaped by their specialisation. However, it is not uncommon for these people to come across real world situations which simply do not fit this world view. A President of the American Economic Association has listed aspects of the "external environment" which are commonly overlooked:

---

[1] Thanks are due to staff of the University of the West of England for helpful comments while visiting on sabbatical, with special thanks to Don Webber for his suggestions, and to Norbert Haering and Helge Peukert for their very constructive comments.
[2] Author contact: k.s.birks@massey.ac.nz
[3] The author has no conflict of interest with any industries/companies/institutions discussed in this paper.

"(1) the framework of legal and political institutions...(2) the complex of social institutions that make up what may loosely be referred to as the social environment; (3) the evolving body of scientific and technical knowledge (and the institutions through which such knowledge is developed and transmitted); (4) the physical environment; and (5) the complex of political and economic arrangements that tie a nation to the rest of the world." (Gordon, 1976)

One response to this cognitive dissonance is for the problem to be largely ignored. This could fit Kuhn's (1970) description of those applying "normal science", or Galbraith's (1999, Chapter 2) of those following the "conventional wisdom". It does little for those seeking an explanation for what they have observed.

My unease with this situation came from experience of policymaking and implementation, including the stated beliefs of those active in these areas. It led me to join the ranks of those looking beyond the conventional economic picture in the hope of finding alternative explanations. It was soon apparent that, outside economics, many of the academics focusing on the *process of policy making* (as opposed to economists identifying policy options) have been critical of what they see as the economics approach. Complex processes in the determination of policy have been described elsewhere. Lindblom described the practice of policy making as "muddling through" (Lindblom, 1959, Lindblom, 1979). Colander has considered such ideas in an economics context, using a similar perspective and terminology (Colander, 2003), but this is essentially on the fringe of economic thinking. Others, as described below, have come from political, news media or other perspectives, often providing very similar suggestions, if from different roots. They suggest that it may be beneficial to consider how rhetorical aspects may influence policy making. Attitudes and public opinion can be shaped, and they are important in the determination of and implementation of policies.

This paper takes the work of Downs (1957) as a starting point for consideration of some aspects of the policy making process. Downs addresses issues in policy making, but subject to restrictive assumptions. He presented a theory of political behaviour, aspects of which have come to be widely acknowledged even among political scientists. To quote Grofman, Downs' work:

"is one of the founding books of the Public Choice movement, and one of the most influential social science books of the twentieth century...[but]

[I]ike most classic works in the social sciences, *An Economic Theory of Democracy* tends to be more cited than read (or reread), and its main ideas have entered the social sciences (especially political science) in only bare bones form."

Downs would not be the first academic to have had convenient aspects of his work adopted while the broader context has been ignored. A similar point has been made on Keynes (Dow, 2012), and Coase also commented on the selective interpretation of his own work (Coase, 1991). Nevertheless, it is paradoxical in that the persistent aspects of his theory (as outlined in section 2 below) are based on assumptions that are standard in economics, but that are rejected by political scientists and that he also recognises as unrealistic. Limited and incorrect information is very important in the real world, but its significance for economic theorising is often overlooked.

This paper outlines key points from Downs' major work on democracy, including the propositions which comprise Grofman's "bare bones". In section 3 it then presents an additional dimension with a discussion on rhetoric and presenting the concept of "macro-rhetoric". Several literature sources are summarised which, collectively, contribute to that concept. Section 4 considers whether the effects of rhetoric might be important for an understanding of economic behaviour. Section 5 builds on this earlier material to derive some alternative propositions along the lines of Downs, but reflecting this broader range of literature from other disciplines. The results are likely to be more consistent with established and accepted thinking in those areas. They may also be more realistic. In concluding, Section 6 presents some implications.

2. Downs' "bare bones"

Anthony Downs presented twenty five "specific testable propositions" in *An Economic Theory of Democracy* (Downs, 1957). These were based on assumptions about the political system, including the motives of politicians as vote maximisers and voters as utility maximisers. In his description he includes detailed consideration of uncertainty and the implications of there being costs associated with information gathering. Despite these being good grounds for misinformation and the use of heuristics, he states, "Throughout this thesis, we assume that no false (i.e. factually incorrect) information exists..." (Downs, 1957). He also states, "Our model in particular ignores all forms of irrationality and subconscious behavior even though they play a vital role in real world politics" (Downs,

1957). These assumptions are commonly found in economics, but they are extreme and may give a distorted view.

Downs presented a basic structure in which voters were well informed. He then extended this to consider partial ignorance and the use by potential voters of party ideology as a substitute for detailed information about party positions on individual issues (Downs, 1957, Chapter 7). This, combined with an assessment of costs and benefits of becoming informed, provided the basis for the suggestion that, if individuals are rational, few would become informed voters. While this was a major focus of attention for political scientists, economists chose to emphasise other aspects of the work. We can see this in the summary provided in Tisdell and Hartley (2008) which highlights three points.

They describe the idea that voters are distributed along a left-to-right political spectrum led to the conclusion that, in a two party system, the parties are likely to take positions near the centre, thus being only narrowly differentiated. This point had been made earlier in the case of the Democratic and Republican parties in the US by Hotelling (1929). The importance of the median voter arises from such thinking, and provides the suggestion that, where this voter is important, redistribution will occur towards the middle of the income distribution. A third prediction is that governments will favour producers over consumers because the former have incentives to be better informed, co-ordinated and resourced.

Downs acknowledges the artificial nature of his two key assumptions, rationality and no false information. Various bodies of literature address issues of rhetoric and political processes, both of which relate to situations where these assumptions may be false. Rhetoric, in particular, involves relaxation of the assumptions, being distinct from logic and hence sometimes resulting in attitudes which would not result from logical reasoning. It is to these aspects that I now turn.

3. "Macro-rhetoric"

A term such as "macro-rhetoric" draws, by analogy, on the economic distinction between microeconomics and macroeconomics. It serves as a unifying concept to bring together traditional rhetoric, which relates to persuasion on a "micro" scale by individuals, commonly in face-to-face contact, and a range of current perspectives on the formation and shaping of social attitudes.

In contrast, modern mainstream economics texts emphasise exogenous preferences. They also assume independently operating decision makers, referred to by

Lawson (2003) and others as atomism.[4] This reflects a significant narrowing of perspective since the early days of economics. Adam Smith (1963) gave a series of lectures on rhetoric in 1762 and 1763. This was not remarkable at the time. Smith reflected a long tradition going back several hundred years in Europe (Serjeantson, 2006) and dating back to classical Greece whereby both logic and rhetoric were considered central to a good education.

Briefly, we could consider logic to be concerned with proof, whereas rhetoric is concerned with persuasion. When describing the rhetoric of political debate, whereby policy decisions are made, Smith used the term "deliberative eloquence". He suggested that it is more likely that people would be persuaded by simple points and rhetorical techniques such as humour, the use of analogy, or appeals to authority or to emotion than by detailed, technical, logical arguments (Smith, 1963). (See Section 3 below for other examples of people making this point.)

Some more recent analyses could be considered as "macro" approaches to rhetoric. So what might be considered in this "macro-rhetoric" literature, and what might it have to offer?

Literature on the processes of policy making can be seen to draw on the scholarship of rhetoric. Dunn presented eleven "modes of argumentation", these being ways in which positions can be presented so as to persuade people to a particular viewpoint (Dunn, 2012).[5] Logic is not mentioned, and his references to standard economics approaches of theory and econometrics might be considered less than complimentary. He lists "method" (techniques such as econometrics) and "cause" (such as economic "laws" based on theory) among his modes, focusing on their use for rhetorical purposes. People may be swayed by arguments couched in those terms, even if the logic is questionable. While this may sound apocryphal to economists, there is some justification for these views. Economic models and theories are not precise

---

[4] This goes back at least to Keynes, who distinguished between atomistic and organic systems: "Keynes...regarded the economic system as being organic. Not only does this involve complex interdependencies over time and space, but also the entire economic system is seen as being open; once we allow for human creativity and caprice, that is, for indeterminism, there is not a closed system waiting to be known." (Dow, 2007) Note also the reference to the longstanding focus on "atomistic competition" in Gordon (1976).

[5] The modes are: i) authority (experts or reference to reports); ii) method (such as econometrics); iii) generalisation (a sample describes the population); iv) classification (ascribed group characteristics); v) cause (as by an economic theory or model); vi) sign (leading economic indicators); vii) motivation (utility maximisation); viii) intuition (an investment guru's gut feeling); ix) analogy-metaphor (government and household budgets);ix) parallel case (country X is doing this); and xi) ethics ("fair and equitable").

representations of the real world, and it has long been argued that there is rhetoric associated with the application of econometrics (McCloskey, 1998, Ziliak and McCloskey, 2008).

This suggests that the results of studies may be convincing, irrespective of the quality of the studies themselves. Persuasive methods include "authority", the use of a source or personality that people trust, and "analogy", applying in one context an approach that people already accept in another (even though it may not, in fact, be suitable). Some of the research techniques that analysts apply may have achieved acceptance on such grounds also. Dunn's "modes of argumentation" suggest that Downs is making overly strong assumptions about the correctness of information and the rationality of individuals. At one point Downs does concede that selective presentation of information may occur, giving scope for some distortion,[6] but the information, albeit partial, is assumed to be accurate.

Other fields are also relevant. In communication literature, "framing" has been described as involving "selection, emphasis, exclusion, and elaboration" (Severin and Tankard, 1997). Choices are made as to what information is relevant and what should be ignored, and what story is told using the selected information. In a series of lectures in 1961 Carr (2008) made the point that historians made choices as to what, out of all the available information, would be "the facts". In economics, given the heavy focus on established models, data series and techniques, this selection is largely prescribed before the researcher even begins the analysis, without the broader selection issue even being considered. This perspective has also been applied to politics, hence:

> "The formal, structural dimension is only one dimension of control over the decision-making process. There is also the more substantive side: policy-makers who take the initiative in **framing** the problem and proposing solutions improve the chances of these solutions being accepted. To this end, the decision-makers may not simply use the force of argument; they may also resort to more manipulative tactics, such as using their monopoly on certain types of policy-relevant information to present their colleagues in the relevant decision units with a highly

---

[6] "Persuaders are not interested *per se* in helping people who are uncertain...they provide only those facts which are favourable to whatever group they are supporting." (Downs, 1957)
For a fictional account with more than a grain of truth, note Lynn & Jay (1989).

stylized picture of the issues involved." (Goldfinch and Hart, 2003)

Literature on critical discourse analysis focuses on the use of selected words to emphasise a particular perspective, and on broader approaches to frame issues in desirable ways. Fairclough (1995) refers to "ideological-discursive formations" (IDFs) which groups may use to define issues and circumscribe debate in a way that favours their perspective. This has been applied in sociology. To quote Hay (1996), "Gramsci's 'war of position' is in fact a war of competing narratives, competing constructions of crisis, increasingly fought out in the media between conflicting political elites." Note also Gramsci's concept of hegemony as described in a study of mass media and politics:

> "Hegemony is a ruling class's (or alliance's) domination of subordinate classes and groups through the elaboration and penetration of ideology (ideas and assumptions) into their common sense and everyday practice; it is the systematic (but not necessarily or even usually deliberate) engineering of mass consent to the established order." (Gitlin, 2003)

Others have suggested that this may be due to passive compliance rather than engineered dominance, and may be inevitable. Viscount Bryce, in a book first published in 1921, stressed the small number of people who actually make the decisions of government, even in a democracy. He contended that those who can influence decisions comprise an "infinitely small" proportion of the population (Bryce, 1929).

Fairclough suggests that a particular IDF may dominate to the exclusion of others (a "dominant IDF"). It can then be seen as the norm, rather than as a particular perspective. Alternatives may then be seen as ideologically driven and biased in comparison to this "true" picture.

Public perceptions and news media presentation of issues will be heavily influenced by dominant terminology and frames. Bertrand Russell made a related point in his essay, "On being open-minded". He was writing in the 1930s (the essay was first published in *The Nation* in 1937) and so he framed his points in the perspective of an earlier generation. Presenting a possible reason why certain language and views may dominate, and why people may choose to conform to these conventions, he wrote:

"The belief that fashion alone should dominate opinion has great advantages. It makes thought unnecessary and puts the highest intelligence within the reach of everyone. It is not difficult to learn the correct use of such words as 'complex', 'sadism', 'Oedipus', 'bourgeois', 'deviation', 'left'; and nothing more is needed to make a brilliant writer or talker…Quite deliberately [the modern-minded man] suppresses what is individual in himself for the sake of the admiration of the herd." (Russell, 1950)

This point was later echoed by Galbraith with his "conventional wisdom" and Kuhn with "normal science". Russell also described the lack of incentive or reward for those who might consider a more independent path.

From the field of public policy, Considine (2005) describes policy as the result of competition between groups, each trying to create the dominant perspective. In a similar vein, other writers on policy process emphasise the setting and denial of groups' agendas (Cobb and Ross, 1997b).

Public perceptions are shaped by the information that is transmitted in these processes, so news media literature may be informative. It might be hoped that debate in the news media would result in an informed public. Bourdieu doubts that this will happen. He suggests that television favours people whom he terms "fast thinkers" (Bourdieu, 1998). These people give quick answers that will be accepted. Far from thinking, they are simply tapping into currently held beliefs, thereby getting instant audience acceptance and giving the appearance of being knowledgeable. His point could apply to much of the mass media. Similarly, to quote someone known for his writing on economics, Galbraith (1999) suggests, "Individuals, most notably the great television and radio commentators, make a profession of knowing and saying with elegance and unction what their audience will find most acceptable". As a consequence, dominant frames are emphasised, prior beliefs reinforced, and false perceptions perpetuated. This can have a significant impact on people's understanding of issues and priorities, at least for those of which they have little or no direct personal experience. This point is made by a political philosopher, Hardin. He uses an appealing term, "street-level epistemology", to describe the way people's "knowledge" on many issues is simply what they have heard and accepted from others, who have in turn heard the information from elsewhere:

"...the bulk of our knowledge...depends on others in various ways. We take most knowledge on authority from others who presumably are in a position to know it. Indeed, we take it from others who themselves take it from others and so forth all the way down. There are finally no or at best vague and weak foundations for most of an individual's knowledge." (Hardin, 2002)

Such information is not checked out. Hence, it is easy for misinformation to spread and false beliefs to be widely accepted. Related concepts include "proof by repeated assertion", the "availability heuristic" (Tversky and Kahneman, 1973), and the concept of "communal reinforcement" (Carroll, 2009). Note also, a principle of advertising by Claude Hopkins that he first published in 1927:

"People are like sheep...We judge things largely by others' impressions, by popular favor...when we see the crowds taking any certain direction, we are much inclined to go with them." (Hopkins, 1998)

Such phenomena are not restricted to the street. University students absorb received wisdom from academics who, in the main, are conveying an accepted body of knowledge. Displacement of dominant bodies of knowledge can be a slow process, even when the body has numerous identified flaws (Desai, 1981, Gellner, 1964, Kuhn, 1970, Lakatos and Musgrave, 1970).

The implications of these processes and phenomena have long been recognised, as described over 150 years ago in *Extraordinary popular delusions and the madness of crowds* (Mackay, 1995). Mackay describes numerous examples that illustrate his point. Current discussion of moral panics supports a contention that every generation has its own popular delusions. Goleman's description of frames and schema further support the view that societies see their world through particular lenses that shape what they see (Goleman, 1997). This serves also as a constraint:

"In all disciplines theory plays a double role: it is both a lens and a blinder. As a lens, it focuses the mind upon specified problems, enabling conditional statements be made about causal relations for a well-defined but limited set of phenomena. But as a blinder, theory narrows the field of vision." (Minsky, 2008)

4. Economics and logic

Mainstream economic theory is based on people having preferences that are fixed, or determined "outside the system/model" (exogenous, rather than endogenous, preferences) (Bowles, 1998). There is then no need to explain preference formation. This simplification is convenient, but not very realistic. There is also an assumption that people are "rational". In this context, this means that, given their preferences and available information, they will act in such a way as to do the best they can according to those preferences. There is a presumption that logic dominates.

There is no place for rhetoric or persuasion in such a view of the world. However, at the most fundamental level, rhetoric is unlikely to have even developed as a separate field of study if people were only persuaded by logical arguments. Schopenhauer presented 38 stratagems for winning arguments. Stratagem No.28 makes the point that a logic-based response to rhetorical criticism would not be effective. Such a defence, "would require a long explanation...and a reference to the principles of the branch of knowledge in question, or to the elements of the matter which you are discussing; and people are not disposed to listen to it" (Schopenhauer, c1851). Politicians seem well aware of the value of well-placed words:

> "Abraham Lincoln...understood the need for simply presented messages. He explained his wish to use the expression, 'The house divided against itself cannot stand', in a major speech in June 1858, 'I want to use some universally known figure expressed in simple language as universally well-known, that may strike home to the minds of men...'" (Herndon and Weik, 1961)

And:

> "Jay Hendrichs argues persuasively that though George W Bush is mocked for his verbal clumsiness, he is actually a highly effective orator. He uses emotive, ethos-laden code words 'without the distraction of logic. He speaks in short sentences, repeating code phrases in effective, if irrational order'." (Leith, 2011)

Given Adam Smith's familiarity with rhetoric, economics appears to have taken a backward step by disregarding this major aspect of policy making and implementation.

Downs was well aware of the simplification and the consequences in terms of a lack of realism. Nevertheless, he based his exposition on two such assumptions.

This approach is understandable on one level. It is relatively easy to model and analyse a purely logical world. Consideration of rhetoric and endogenous preferences presents major problems for the use of many commonly applied economic methods of evaluation. How are economists to determine costs and benefits if the values that are observed through either actual behaviour or elicitation through surveys, etc., can be influenced by rhetoric and false or misleading information? This is a major limitation to the value of much economic analysis for decision making. Tacit acceptance of the analyses as providing accurate values to use in policy evaluation contributes to the rhetoric of economics.

The swaying of opinions and spread of inaccurate beliefs are likely to be of particular relevance where two conditions hold: first, when the issues are those about which individuals have little or no direct involvement, so their opinions are not shaped by first-hand experience; and second, where the issues require collective action, so that there is little benefit to an individual from acquiring an accurate understanding. These conditions apply for many policy issues. Cobb and Ross (1997a) describe initial problem "identification groups" which attempt to raise awareness and achieve change. There is a requirement that they gain the support of much larger "attention groups" if an issue is to gain a place on the policy agenda. Cobb and Ross also describe mechanisms whereby the agendas of less powerful groups can be denied. These dimensions suggest a dynamics to political processes that cannot be addressed by assuming fixed preferences.

Lakoff and Johnson, in a key text, emphasise the importance of metaphor, suggesting that our perceptions can be distorted because much of our understanding arises indirectly. Hence:

> "...many aspects of our experience cannot be clearly delineated in terms of the naturally emergent dimensions of our experience. This is typically the case for human emotions, abstract concepts, mental activity, time, work, human institutions, social practices, etc....Though most of these can be *experienced* directly, none of them can be fully comprehended on their own terms. Instead, we must understand them in terms of other entities and experiences, typically other *kinds* of entities and experiences." (Lakoff and Johnson, 2003.)

This quote suggests that our actual perceptions are a synthesis of objective and subjective aspects. They make the point that objectivism misses the fact that understanding depends on how the world is framed, and subjectivism misses the fact that framing, or a "conceptual system" "is grounded in our successful functioning in our physical and cultural environments" (Lakoff and Johnson, 2003). This last point may explain why there can be greater problems with policy and implementation issues, as they are less closely associated with our individual functioning.

Downs' approach was to present several propositions that were plausible given his assumptions. The following section takes a similar approach, but relaxes Downs' assumptions on rationality and the absence of false information, hence assuming a "macro-rhetoric" environment.

5. Downs with traction

Traction is a term frequently used by politicians and in the news media to indicate that an issue has attention. It is not a precisely defined term, although it has acquired widespread usage and acceptance. Its applicability in particular instances arises from a perception or belief by decision makers that the issue has assumed sufficient prominence in terms of concern by relevant people. It could be considered to indicate that an issue has been placed on an agenda, as in agenda setting and denial (Cobb and Ross, 1997a). While a precise definition would be preferable, loose recognition of a characteristic in this way is not unknown (Rawls, 2001, Goffman, 1974).

The concept of traction is important when considering policy success. Points can be made, and evidence presented, but without traction there is unlikely to be the interest or support for an issue to gain a prominent position on a policy agenda. Even if an issue is important to a dominant political party, the party risks unpopularity and resistance if it proceeds without popular acceptance. There is a close association with rhetoric, both micro and macro, in that these latter consider how people can be persuaded to see issues in particular ways. The need for traction is a constraint on political activity, and it also suggests an arena in which political contests take place. The following general points and associated propositions are not comprehensive. Rather, they are an attempt to indicate, in a Downs-like framework, some of the important implications of this activity. They have been derived from direct experience of policy formulation and political debate, evaluated in the context of the bodies of literature outlined above.

5.1 A limited number of issues

The operation of the news media and the importance of "traction" suggest that Downs' approach could be modified to consider agenda-setting and the shaping of observed preferences. For the purposes of an exploratory investigation, consider the possibility that there can only be a limited number of policy issues on the agenda at any one time. There are broad reasons for this. Simon, on "attention scarcity", writes, "...a wealth of information creates a poverty of attention and a need to allocate that attention efficiently among the overabundance of information sources that might consume it" (Simon, 1971). Take as an example a basic economic assessment. There are costs of gathering and processing information, and there are, at least initially, economies of scale in gathering information on specific issues. The news media are important for the transmission of this information, and they influence the number of issues addressed and the quality and nature of information presented. This point is discussed further in Birks (2008). Also, Hardin's concept of "street-level epistemology" suggests that people take their knowledge from others without much individual critical assessment (Hardin, 2002). This is closely linked to critical discourse analysis (CDA), whereby the form of presentation of information shapes people's perceptions. As items on the political agenda require co-ordinated action, it is generally not enough for interested individuals to develop a degree of understanding on their own. However, it is easy to "overload" the system:

"Large public problems...periodically require a synchrony of public attention. This is more than enough to crowd the agenda to the point of unworkability or inaction" (Simon, 1971).

The general public may only be willing or able to consider a few options at a time, but politicians who wish to set agendas will also seek to limit the options available for discussion. Whatever the reason, it has been observed that "...for any problem at the regime or macro-level of discussion and analysis **there are remarkably few alternatives actually under debate**" (Bosso, 1994). Similarly (original emphasis), "There are billions of potential conflicts in any modern society, but *only a few become significant*" (Schattschneider, 1960).

Consequently it is plausible to suggest that issues are not set by individual voters, as might be assumed in economic theory based on atomistic individuals each with their own exogenous preferences. Rather, it may be more realistic to consider them set by politicians, pressure groups and the news media, after which individuals form their opinions. This may be a large adjustment for formal models as commonly used in economics. However, in a general description without restrictive assumptions it is only a small step. The result is that it opens up the possibility of a synthesis of the approaches. This gives a first proposition under a traction approach:

Proposition 1: There are a limited number of issues with traction at any one time.

5.2 Parties competing for traction

Parties select issues either because they fit their policy agenda or because they believe that they will win votes. If an issue has traction, it has public attention. Consequently, voters are likely to believe that something should be done about it. Hence there will be voter support for policies that are perceived to be addressing issues with traction. As parties are competing against each other, their aim is to achieve traction on their issues, but not on those of other parties. This is central to the themes of agenda setting and denial (Cobb and Ross, 1997b), where agenda denial limits the traction on denied issues. Hence the claim, "the definition of the alternatives is the supreme instrument of power" (Schattschneider, 1960). This gives a second proposition:

Proposition 2: Parties aim to achieve traction on their issues and prevent traction on others.

Whereas Downs takes the policy environment and agenda issues as given, an analysis which focuses more on rhetoric and policy process recognises that these are fluid and contestable. Proposition 2 can be developed with additional sub-themes which consider possible strategies in a dynamic political policy environment. Downs' second proposition is that, "Both parties in a two-party system agree on any issues that a majority of citizens strongly favor" (Downs, 1957). A traction perspective would require two steps to get to this stage. First, an issue must have traction, and second, there must be both consensus on the required policy approach and little chance that alternative policies could gain acceptance. This recognises that there are not only priorities on issues, but also on choice of policy instruments.[7] This suggests the following sub-themes:

2a) Parties have policies on issues with traction (but the policies need not be the same).

It is harder to generate traction for a new issue than to present policies for an issue that already has traction. Also, there is a limited number of issues with traction, but numerous other issues which are not receiving attention. It can be difficult to focus attention on a new issue at the expense of prevailing recognised concerns. This might explain why more attention may be given to the process of achieving and maintaining awareness than to debate on the details of policy issues, options and responses (rhetorical matters rather than analysis). Hence:

2b) Parties are more likely to invest in an issue with traction than to generate traction for a new issue.

Besides agenda denial strategies, there can be conspiracies of silence to overcome, "...whereby people tacitly agree to publicly ignore something of which they are all personally aware" (Zerubavel, 2007). This is further illustrated:

> "Watching Peter disregard a distinctly audible comment...may lead Paul to consider it irrelevant and thereby disregard it as well, yet watching Paul also ignore it may in turn reinforce Peter's initial impression that it was indeed irrelevant. We basically have here a vicious cycle" (Zerubavel, 2007).

This could extend to the entire realm of political matters, which, as Eliasoph (1998) described, can become a taboo subject within a social network due to the social riskiness of voicing political opinions. This phenomenon has been more generally described as the 'elephant in the room'. So society, or groups in society, may fail to discuss significant policy issues. In general, this is unlikely to be rectified through the news media, which aim to appeal to the public and therefore focus on issues that are known to be of interest, as discussed further below. Hence:

---

[7] Weaver (2007) talks about first- and second-level agenda setting, with the first relating to "what" and the second to "how". He sees second-level agenda setting as relating to framing.

2c) The media tend to reinforce the prevailing pattern of issues with traction.

Sowell (2004) suggests that organisations initially established to promote affirmative action face inbuilt pressures to grow. The same could apply to organizations more generally. Hence organizations can be expected to build on existing traction, seeking new dimensions for their issues so as to have a continuing reason to exist. Similar points are made by Schattschneider (1960) and in literature on historical institutionalism. Hence:

2d) Institutions that have been established due to an issue with traction aim to maintain that traction through expansion of the issue.

5.3 Shifting public opinion and development of traction

Many policy issues are beyond the scope of individual action, and therefore have received little individual attention. Concern for such issues depends in part on the concern expressed by others. If something is considered by many to be important, more people will invest time and emotional energy into being concerned. Cobb and Ross would say that an issue has successfully spread beyond the "identification group", being understood by the "attentive public" and adopted by some of the "attention groups" (Cobb and Ross, 1997a). Hardin (2002) might suggest that the position is spread through street-level epistemology. In this sense, traction is "cumulative". It can involve misinformation, the development and exploitation of 'factoids' (Pruden, 2007), and other rhetorical stratagems.

Proposition 3: Traction can build on itself.

However, there can be a time limit on this. Downs (1972), writing some years after the publication of his theory, hypothesised that many issues are subject to an "issue attention cycle", whereby interest and support can be generated for a time among members of the wider community.

Competition to generate and maintain traction can be described further. When the government promotes a particular issue or position, there is an associated framing of the issue and a belief that something can be done about it. Also, there is perhaps a natural tendency for people to align themselves with the prevailing authority as described by Strentz, who writes of, "the common occurrence of people adopting the values and beliefs of a new government to avoid social retaliation and punishment" (Strentz, 2005). In part, these effects may arise because issues closely related to the government are more newsworthy, especially if fronted by official spokespeople who thereby lend their authority to the positions they take. "Officialness makes the news statist, that is, it contributes to a tendency to cover state voices rather than civil ones..." (Schudson, 2003). There may also be important 'processes of attitude change' to consider. This suggests the following sub-theme:

3a) The public will tend to move in favour of policies promoted by the current government.

Traction can be important in other ways also, suggesting two additional sub-themes. If traction is the key to success in getting policies adopted, then it will be a major focus for political parties. Rhetorical strategies will be used to achieve traction. Reasoned analysis and argument may not be required. In fact, reason can be counter-productive if it is less likely to attract public attention than other approaches more suited to the prevailing news media. Instead, careful choice of language, or framing, has been advocated for the New Zealand Labour Party in terms that echo Downs' reference to ideology:

> "Use language to create identity...Create an identity for Labour that mirrors positive core values of decent New Zealanders – so that people know what Labour is without having to talk about issues" (Curran, 2006).

A similar approach towards the climate change debate is described by Broder (2009). Even among politicians, simple presentation of issues may be preferred. Then it is easier to obtain consensus and to present policy proposals in a clear and convincing way. Keynes (1937) was aware of this when he wrote, "There is nothing a government hates more than to be well-informed; for it makes the process of arriving at decisions much more complicated and difficult". Hence:

3b) It is easier to generate traction through authority, celebrity support or framing than through detailed, informed presentation of information.

If an issue has traction, then it may provide more persuasive grounds than valid, reasoned argument as a basis for a policy change. For example, the New Zealand government raised nurses' pay in 2006 on the basis that, as a woman-dominated occupation, there must have been discrimination against them resulting in low pay. This argument was used in preference to a probably sounder (economics/market-forces based) case that the prevailing rates of pay were insufficient to overcome a nursing shortage. The discrimination argument suited and reinforced the position presented in Department of Labour and Human Rights Commission documents (Crossan, 2004, Mintrom and True, 2004). This may have been an easier way to obtain the desired result, and it served to reinforce the broader issue, thus giving wider political benefits. A clear example of false claims to support a desired policy is that of Saddam Hussein and possession of weapons of mass destruction (Maddow, 2013).

3c) An issue with traction may be used as a false justification for a policy rather than a more logically-based alternative.

5.4 The importance of process

A major focus of politicians' attention is on obtaining and maintaining public support, publicly measured by relative performance in the polls. This is necessary, if only for political survival. Downs describes his model as being "based on the assumption that every government seeks to maximise political support" (Downs, 1957). This is then interpreted as vote-maximisation (Downs, 1957). Given the importance of rhetoric, and arguably a need for apparently decisive government, there is limited scope for open, logical policy development with detailed consideration and evaluation of the options. Instead, the actual policy direction may have already been decided, and the requirement is then simply to follow expected processes (such as consultation, and possibly public submissions) (March and Olsen, 1989). Tyler (2000), writing on 'procedural justice', describes this in terms of the importance of process as a basis for legitimacy of decisions, and people's willingness to accept the results if the required processes are followed. We could consider this as another heuristic, along with party ideology. March and Olsen also refer to the importance of process and limited concern for outcomes in political deliberation. Information is required to symbolise and signal "decision making propriety", and intentions are more important than outcomes for legitimacy (March and Olsen, 1989).

Proposition 4: The focus in politics is more on the process of policy change than on accurate, informed debate on a range of options and the determination of desirable policies.

This suggests a context in which there are reasons to limit monitoring and policy revision. Governments aim to implement their agendas. Parties in opposition attempt to obstruct governments. One way to do this is to identify problems that can be presented as government's failures and needing urgent attention, thereby drawing political resources away from the planned agenda. Opposition parties may also attempt to get traction for their own agenda items. Monitoring generates attention. Detailed monitoring provides information that can detract from a government's agenda and give ammunition for opposition parties. Given the limited number of issues on the agenda at any one time (see Proposition 1), such distractions can be costly to governments. It is therefore in a government's interest to allow as little attention as possible to be given to existing policies/laws. Revision of laws will only occur when problems are noticeable enough, and generate sufficient interest by attention groups, to gain traction. Hence:

4a) A government will attempt to limit monitoring so as to minimise attention given to issues that are not on its agenda.

4b) Once a law has been passed, it is unlikely to be evaluated or reconsidered for many years.

6. Implications

Briefly stated, Downs applied an approach under the general umbrella of static analysis as commonly seen in mainstream economics. Consequently the focus was on **outcomes** with limited ability to consider **process**. The additional dimensions outlined above draw on literature which focuses on process. This could be considered as an extension of Downs, including process and relaxing his key assumptions of rationality and no false information. Alternatively, it could be viewed as an attempt to synthesise two bodies of literature.

This paper has presented a concept of 'macro-rhetoric' and derived a set of propositions building from a range of literature beyond the normal bounds of economics. While this literature may use different terms applied in various contexts, collectively they fall under the broad umbrella of rhetoric, how and why people come to see things as they do.

There is a marked difference between these approaches and the behavioural assumptions of mainstream economics. Economics based on exogenous preferences inevitably ignores rhetoric, with its focus on persuasion. The exogeneity assumption suggests that people's valuations simply exist and are available to be measured and used for policy evaluation. This option disappears once endogeneity is acknowledged, inevitably limiting the value of economic analysis, especially in areas involving deliberation on indirect or collective policy issues.

Within economics there is one theoretical, idealised approach to policy making that can be described as follows. If there is free, perfect information (a parallel to the zero transaction cost assumption), then all possible policy alternatives can be considered. For each alternative, all the costs and benefits can be identified and measured. The optimal policy can then be selected using an appropriate decision rule.

Even without consideration of costs of analysis with its associated requirements of information and expertise, an economic approach may not be politically feasible due to competing groups and agendas and the rhetoric of political discourse. In such an environment, parties select their preferred policies, after which they operate in a political arena to put their policies into practice. Detailed scrutiny at this late stage would generally be unwelcome, especially where it involves consideration of numerous alternative options (including those of opposition parties). Economists should therefore be aware of the constraints on policy determination arising from the political process. To quote Simon:

> "The dream of thinking everything out before we act, of making certain we have all the facts and know all the consequences, is…the dream of someone with no appreciation of the seamless web of causation, the limits of human thinking, or the scarcity of human attention." (Simon, 1971)

As has been discussed in this paper, in disciplines other than economics a range of concepts, collectively "macro-rhetoric", are emphasised. In particular, framing, the choice of language and promotion of key terms, and agenda setting and denial are considered by some outside economics to be central components of political and social activity. Hardin's "street-level epistemology", along with Mackay's popular delusions, also suggests that at times viewpoints and ideas can become widely accepted without being strongly justified.[8] Processes whereby groups may be motivated to become active are described by Cobb and Ross, Schattschneider and others.

This paper indicates some of the possibilities when Downs' approach is taken together with some of the points in the policy-related literature. As shown, it is possible to develop alternative propositions which incorporate concepts and observations from a broad range of academic literature and which provide arguably a far more realistic representation of the policy making process. The propositions that are presented above collectively paint an interesting picture of an environment in which people are persuaded to subscribe to particular viewpoints and policy decisions are made. While any theoretical viewpoint is merely describing an analogous structure to the real world, it may be emphasising some aspects which are important.

The picture is one of a limited number of issues commanding attention at any one time, with groups and parties competing to control or influence the agenda. Where an issue has enough attention to gain traction, parties will take a position on that issue. They are less likely to try to promote a new issue, and the news media will generally focus on issues which have already achieved traction. Where institutions have been established in relation to an issue, those institutions have an incentive to promote and broaden the issue. Public opinion tends to follow issues that are seen to have wider support or are supported by the current government. It is guided not so much by reasoned debate as by authority, celebrity endorsement and framing. Plausible arguments may be used when they are persuasive and politically desirable even though they may not stand up to rigorous scrutiny. The political focus, as described in the relevant political literature, tends to be more on agenda setting and denial, competing for public attention and political support on issues, rather than on deliberation on policy options. Governments will not wish to have attention drawn to issues that are not on the agenda, including laws that have been passed, and so monitoring on these matters will not be encouraged.

The implications for policy are important. There are clear possibilities of failure in the policy making process and errors may not be identified for many years. Consequently it may be productive for analysis to consider two responses. First, potential limitations in the political process should be recognised. Second, as limitations of the process are also limitations in policy formulation and implementation, resulting constraints on the potential

---

[8] This possibility has also be suggested in relation to economics: "While the deficiencies of the orthodox approach may not be clearcut in the case of every one of the subtopics surveyed, the overall critique of neoclassical theory as a coherent explanation of how a modern, technologically advanced economy functions is a devastating one. The wonder is that scholars continue to propound it and that statesmen continue to accept advice based on it." (Eichner, 1979)

effectiveness of policies should be recognised. Economists' policy recommendations should not simply reflect the requirements of an ideal structure within which atomistic private sector decision makers then operate. Their recommendations are, in practice, feeding into a complex system of deliberation and persuasion that shapes both choice of policies and outcomes in terms of policy implementation. This would suggest that economists may be able to make a valuable contribution by following actual policy debate more closely. Their research and public presentation of findings could then be aimed directly at improving the level of understanding of economic aspects of policy decisions and increasing critical commentary and monitoring of policies. Results could then also be placed in a context in which their value can be readily appreciated by the wider community.

References

Birks, S. 2008. The Media and an informed electorate - an economist's perspective. *In:* Tilley, E. (ed.) *Power & place: refereed proceedings of the Australian & New Zealand Communication Association Conference, Wellington, July 9-11.* Wellington: ANZCA.

Bosso, C. J. 1994. The contextual basis of problem definition. *In:* Rochefort, D. A. & Cobb, R. W. (eds.) *The politics of problem definition: shaping the policy agenda.* Lawrence, Kan.: University Press of Kansas.

Bourdieu, P. 1998. *On television,* New York, New Press.

Bowles, S. 1998. Endogenous preferences: the cultural consequences of markets and other economic institutions. *Journal of Economic Literature,* 36, 75-111.

Broder, J. M. 2009. Seeking to save the planet, with a thesaurus. *The New York Times,* 1 May.

Bryce, J. 1929. *Modern democracies,* London, Macmillan.

Carr, E. H. 2008. *What is history?,* Harmondsworth, Penguin.

Carroll, R. T. 2009. *Communal reinforcement* [Online]. Available: http://skepdic.com/comreinf.html [Accessed 13 March 2009.

Coase, R. H. 1991. *The institutional structure of production - Nobel Prize lecture* [Online]. Available: http://nobelprize.org/nobel_prizes/economics/laureates/1991/coase-lecture.html [Accessed 21 October 2013.

Cobb, R. W. & Ross, M. H. 1997a. Agenda setting and the denial of agenda access: key concepts. *In:* Cobb, R. W. & Ross, M. H. (eds.) *Cultural strategies of agenda denial: Avoidance, attack, and redefinition.* Lawrence: University Press of Kansas.

Cobb, R. W. & Ross, M. H. (eds.) 1997b. *Cultural strategies of agenda denial: avoidance, attack, and redefinition,* Lawrence: University Press of Kansas.

Colander, D. 2003. Muddling through and policy analysis. *In:* Birks, S. (ed.) *Economics and policy - worlds apart?* Palmerston North: Centre for Public Policy Evaluation, Massey University.

Considine, M. 2005. *Making public policy: institutions, actors, strategies,* Cambridge, Polity Press.

Crossan, D. 2004. Report of the taskforce on: pay and employment equity in the public service and the public health and public education sectors. *In:* Labour, D. o. (ed.). Department of Labour.

Curran, C. 2006. Language matters: setting agendas - taking charge of the language *Otago/Southland Labour Party regional conference.*

Desai, M. 1981. *Testing monetarism,* London, Pinter.

Dow, S. C. 2007. Variety of methodological approach in economics. *Journal of Economic Surveys,* 21**,** 447-465.

Dow, S. C. 2012. *Foundations for new economic thinking: a collection of essays,* Houndmills, Basinstoke, Hampshire, Palgrave Macmillan.

Downs, A. 1957. *An economic theory of democracy,* New York, Harper.

Downs, A. 1972. Up and down with ecology: the issue attention cycle. *Public Interest***,** 38-50.

Dunn, W. N. 2012. *Public policy analysis : an introduction,* Boston, Pearson.

Eichner, A. S. 1979. A look ahead. *In:* Eichner, A. S. (ed.) *A guide to Post-Keynesian economics.* White Plains, N.Y.: Sharp.

Eliasoph, N. 1998. *Avoiding politics: how Americans produce apathy in everyday life,* Cambridge, UK, Cambridge University Press.

Fairclough, N. 1995. *Critical discourse analysis: the critical study of language,* London, Longman.

Galbraith, J. K. 1999. *The affluent society,* London, Penguin.

Gellner, E. 1964. *Thought and change,* London, Weidenfeld and Nicolson.

Gitlin, T. 2003. *The whole world is watching: mass media in the making & unmaking of the New Left,* Berkeley, Calif., University of California Press.

Goffman, E. 1974. *Frame analysis: an essay on the organization of experience,* Cambridge, Mass., Harvard University Press.

Goldfinch, S. & Hart, P. t. 2003. Leadership and institutional reform: engineering macroeconomic policy change in Australia. *Governance,* 16**,** 235-270.

Goleman, D. 1997. *Vital lies, simple truths: the psychology of self-deception,* London, Bloomsbury.

Gordon, R. A. 1976. Rigor and relevance in a changing institutional setting. *The American Economic Review,* 66**,** 1-14.

Hardin, R. 2002. Street-level epistemology and democratic participation. *Journal of Political Philosophy,* 10**,** 212-229.

Hay, C. 1996. Narrating crisis: the discursive construction of the 'winter of discontent'. *Sociology,* 30**,** 253-277.

Herndon, W. H. & Weik, J. W. 1961. *Herndon's life of Lincoln: the history and personal recollections of Abraham Lincoln as originally written by William H. Herndon and Jesse W. Weik,* Greenwich, Fawcett.

Hopkins, C. C. 1998. *My life in advertising & Scientific advertising: two works,* Chicago, NTC Business Books.

Hotelling, H. 1929. Stability in competition. *The Economic Journal,* 39, 41-57.

Keynes, J. M. 1937. Borrowing for defence: is it inflation? A plea for organized policy. *The Times,* 11 March, p.17.

Kuhn, T. S. 1970. *The structure of scientific revolutions,* Chicago, University of Chicago Press.

Lakatos, I. & Musgrave, A. (eds.) 1970. *Criticism and the growth of knowledge,* London: Cambridge University Press.

Lakoff, G. & Johnson, M. 2003. *Metaphors we live by,* Chicago, Ill., University of Chicago Press.

Lawson, T. 2003. *Reorienting economics,* London, Routledge.

Leith, S. 2011. You talkin' to me?: Rhetoric from Aristotle to Obama. London: Profile Books.

Lindblom, C. E. 1959. The science of "muddling through". *Public Administration Review,* 19, 79-88.

Lindblom, C. E. 1979. Still muddling, not yet through. *Public Administration Review,* 39, 517-526.

Lynn, J. & Jay, A. 1989. *The complete Yes Prime Minister: The diaries of the Right Hon. James Hacker,* London, BBC Books.

Mackay, C. 1995. *Extraordinary popular delusions and the madness of crowds,* Ware, Wordsworth Editions.

Maddow, R. 2013. *Hubris: selling the Iraq war [video, part 1 no longer available]* [Online]. Available: http://video.msnbc.msn.com/rachel-maddow/50852099#50852121 [Accessed 30 September 2013.

March, J. G. & Olsen, J. P. 1989. *Rediscovering institutions: the organisational basis of politics,* New York, Free Press.

McCloskey, D. N. 1998. *The rhetoric of economics,* Madison, Wis., University of Wisconsin Press.

Minsky, H. P. 2008. *Stabilizing an unstable economy,* New York, McGraw-Hill.

Mintrom, M. & True, J. 2004. Framework for the future: equal employment opportunities in New Zealand. Wellington: Human Rights Commission.

Pruden, W. 2007. Ah, there's joy in Mudville's precincts. *The Washington Times,* 23 January.

Rawls, J. 2001. *Justice as fairness: a restatement,* Cambridge, Mass., Harvard University Press.

Russell, B. 1950. *Unpopular essays,* New York, Simon and Schuster.

Schattschneider, E. E. 1960. *The semisovereign people; a realist's view of democracy in America,* New York, Holt, Rinehart and Winston.

Schopenhauer, A. c1851. The art of controversy.

Schudson, M. 2003. *The sociology of news,* New York, Norton.

Serjeantson, R. W. 2006. Proof and persuasion. *In:* Park, K. & Daston, L. (eds.) *The Cambridge history of science: Volume 3 - Early modern science.* Cambridge: Cambridge University Press.

Severin, W. J. & Tankard, J. W. 1997. *Communication theories: origins, methods, and uses in the mass media,* New York, Longman.

Simon, H. A. 1971. Designing organisations for an information-rich world. *In:* Greenberger, M. (ed.) *Computers, communications, and the public interest.* Baltimore: The Johns Hopkins Press.

Smith, A. 1963. *Lectures on rhetoric and belles lettres: delivered in the University of Glasgow by Adam Smith, reported by a student in 1762-63,* London, Nelson.

Sowell, T. 2004. *Affirmative action around the world: an empirical study,* New Haven, Yale UP.

Strentz, T. 2005. *Psychological aspects of crisis negotiation,* Boca Raton, FL, Taylor & Francis.

Tisdell, C. A. & Hartley, K. 2008. *Microeconomic policy: a new perspective,* Cheltenham, UK, Edward Elgar.

Tversky, A. & Kahneman, D. 1973. Availability: a heuristic for judging frequency and probability. *Cognitive Psychology,* 5, 207-232.

Tyler, T. R. 2000. Social justice: outcome and procedure. *International Journal of Psychology,* 35, 117-125.

Weaver, D. H. 2007. Thoughts on agenda setting, framing, and priming. *Journal of Communication,* 57, 142-147.

Zerubavel, E. 2007. The social structure of denial. *In:* Reed, I. & Alexander, J. C. (eds.) *Culture, society, and democracy: the interpretive approach.* Boulder: Paradigm Publishers.

Ziliak, S. T. & McCloskey, D. N. 2008. *The cult of statistical significance: how the standard error costs us jobs, justice, and lives,* Ann Arbor, MI, University of Michigan Press.

How the Culture of Economics Stops Economists from Studying Group Behavior and the Development of Social Cultures

Hendrik Van den Berg[1]
Department of Economics, University of Nebraska, USA

Abstract

Economic thought evolved over the past two centuries to focus on individual behavior as the basis for all economic activity. Some heterodox economists have pointed to the importance of group behavior and the influence of organizations on economic activity, but the neoclassical paradigm, with the rational isolated individual as its main actor, prevails in mainstream economics. This paper presents a "sociology of economics" to explain why the culture of the field of economics effectively blinds its practitioners to the phenomenon of group behavior. Drawing on the work of Pierre Bourdieu, the paper details the field's methodology (habitus), which includes the assumptions of the rational and separable individual, and the belief system (doxa), consisting of the metaphors of the invisible hand and rational free choice, that supports the habitus. The culture of economics is firmly held in place by symbolic violence directed at those who question the prevailing culture. The paper further highlights the role of business and financial interests in supporting the prevailing culture of economics. In conclusion, a strong group culture, supported by powerful business and financial organizations, discourages economists from recognizing this group culture or the powerful organizations that support it.

Keywords: Culture, neoclassical economics, orthodoxy, pluralism, sociology

"Homo oeconomicus, as conceived (tacitly or explicitly) by economic orthodoxy, is a kind of anthropological monster: this theoretically minded man of practice is the most extreme personification of the scholastic fallacy, an intellectualist or intellectualocentric error very common in the social sciences, by which the scholar puts into the heads of the agents he is studying – housewives or households, firms or entrepreneurs, etc. –

---

[1] Professor of Economics, Department of Economics, University of Nebraska, Lincoln, NE 68588-0489, USA; Telephone: (402) 472-2319; email: hvan-den-berg1@unl.edu; Adjunct Professor, University of Missouri at Kansas City.

the theoretical considerations and constructions he has had to develop in order to account for their practices." Pierre Bourdieu (2005b, p. 209).

1. Introduction

Mainstream economists in nearly all Western countries use almost exclusively neoclassical models in their work. Neoclassical models usually assume that economic actors are all rational individuals who take only their own material well-being into consideration when they make economic choices. The practical benefit of such assumptions is that aggregate economic activity can be described as the mathematical sum of its component parts, assuming also, of course, that the system remains unchanged. Often such models are reduced to *representative agent* models, in which one average *economic person*, or *homo oeconomicus* in Bourdieu's quote above, represents aggregate economic behavior. This modeling strategy is reminiscent of Margaret Thatcher's suggestion that "there is no society, just individuals." This approach to economic modeling not only makes it difficult to analyze the economic behavior of organizations and other forms of group behavior, but it also misrepresents how real people behave.

Mainstream economics' assumption that humans act and make decisions in isolation is not consistent with what psychologists, sociologists, political scientists, behavioral economists, and other social scientists know about human behavior. There is ample evidence that humans are group animals who exhibit feelings toward others, such as envy and empathy, and enter into a variety of social relationships. Humans are not isolationists. Among the many costs of the intellectual mistake of placing an unrealistically individualistic and self-centered *homo eoconomicus* at the center of economic analysis is that it prevents economists from analyzing the important economic roles of groups and organizations. The behavior of business firms, labor unions, government agencies, and lobby groups, among many other organizations, cannot be explained as a sum of the actions of their individual members. Also, the emphasis on the individual makes it difficult for mainstream economists to analyze the development of social phenomena such as institutions and culture. According to mainstream economic thinking, there is no such thing as a group culture, only rational self-centered individual behavior. Hence, even when they do recognize the importance of cultures and other formal institutions in shaping economic behavior, mainstream economists usually enter these group phenomena into their models as exogenous variables that the individual actors are then assumed to adjust to in a rational manner along with various other exogenous and endogenous economic variables.

This paper seeks an explanation for why the field of economics restricts the scope of its analysis to the point where its practitioners often ignore or, at best, mis-specify the economic roles of clearly identifiable groups and organizations as well as group phenomena like culture. This paper argues that the explanation lies in the field's culture, one of those group phenomena that mainstream economists cannot easily deal with. Psychologists, behavioral economists, and neuroscientists, among others, have documented how humans develop cultures in order to deal with the extraordinary complexity of their existence. In short, group phenomena such as institutions and culture are endogenous to all human decision making and thus all economic behavior. While culture can help establish common patterns of behavior that help people go about their daily lives, culture can also distort reality and mislead people. The culture of economics is a case in point, as it has led economists to ignore important economic issues related to organizations and group phenomena.

This paper draws on other fields, especially sociology, for an explanation of the culture of economics. Specifically, the work of the French sociologist Pierre Bourdieu provides a useful framework for understanding why economists developed and sustain a culture that effectively makes is difficult for economists to study the causes and consequences of organized group behavior in economies. The paper concludes with some comments on how economists can escape their restrictive culture and more effectively study the organizations that play such a dominant role in every modern economy. Overall, it will be very difficult for the field of economics to escape from its well-established culture of individualism, especially because this culture prevents economists from seriously recognizing the shortcomings of its own culture.

2. Some history of economic thought

A major barrier to a better understanding of group behavior and the economic role of organizations is economists' embrace of the unsound modeling strategy known as *scientific reductionism*. This modeling approach assumes that it is possible to understand the whole system simply by analyzing the individual parts in isolation. By engaging in scientific reductionism, economists ignore the possibility that the whole economic system, or large sectors of the economy, generate outcomes that depend not only on the parts, but also how the parts interact. They thus ignore the possibility that some economic systems may work better than others even though they have the similar sets of people and natural resources to work with.

The widespread acceptance of scientific reductionism dates from the latter half of the nineteenth century, when economists began to focus on resource allocation within the narrow confines of an economy's market sector. Economists effectively began to assume, as most mainstream or orthodox neoclassical economists still do today, that a good understanding of the economic system's market sector was sufficient for designing economic policies and institutions. Not only were household activities, interactions with nature, and other non-market activities ignored, but the potential for systemic booms and busts were ruled out in the neoclassical models that hypothesized smooth functions and stable market equilibria within a static, unchanging system.

The best-selling economics textbook beginning in 1890 was Marshall's *Principles of Economics*, the eighth edition of which was published in 1920. Even though Marshall recognized in passing many aspects of economic complexity, the dominant scientific reductionist modeling strategy of his textbook effectively established the neoclassical paradigm that still dominates mainstream economics. Of special historical significance is Walras' (1874) model, which specified an economy as a large system of linear equations, one for demand and one for supply in each of the millions of markets where consumers purchased goods and services from producers, governments purchased goods and services from producers, producers purchased capital goods from other producers, producers purchased labor from individuals, and producers rented land from landowners. Walras specified a system with m products, m product prices, m product quantities, n factors of production, n factor prices, n factor quantities, and mn technical coefficients. In general, a system of linear equations can be solved if the number of unknowns is equal to the number of equations, and Walras' satisfied that requirement. However, the model was too large for economists to actually use for practical analysis.

Walras' huge mathematical model seemed to reflect the complex nature of an economic system in which all of the many parts were linked to all other parts. But, in order to project the idea that the economy was a stable, solvable system, Walras assumed a system of linear equations with fixed parameters, which implied that the relationships among the component parts of the system could not vary. His model, therefore, did not represent a realistic economic system in which variations in which both component parts and the relationships among the component parts change over time. And, given that Walras set individuals up as the actors in his linear and additive system of markets, the formation of independent and unique groups and organizations of consumers, producers, workers, etc. was ruled out.

Ironically, because economists intuitively accepted that there was a solution to Walras' system of equations but were unable to actually apply the huge Walrasian model to deal with practical problems, they felt justified to focus on individual markets and ignore the interconnections within the overall system. This flight to *scientific reductionism* even revived Smith's (1776) metaphor of the invisible hand, which suggested that as long as the individual mn markets functioned well, overall economic outcomes were always socially optimal. The ideas associated with Walras, Marshall, and other late nineteenth century economists who implicitly accepted scientific reductionism along with the central role of the rational individual is known as the *neoclassical school*.

The scientific reductionist tendencies in economics were suddenly reversed in the 1930s, when the world economy plunged into the Great Depression. Clearly, the economic system was not stable or constant, and the same set of people, machines, infrastructure, and natural resources generated very different outcomes in 1929 and 1930. For several decades, macroeconomic policies were influenced by Keynes' (1936) *General Theory of Employment, Interest, and Money*, a work that contradicted the invisible hand by showing why the systemic interactions among different groups in society were likely to generate and sustain economic recessions and depressions. Keynesian analysis also suggested that the actions of distinctive groups of economic actors had large consequences on the overall economic system and, therefore, the welfare of everyone in the system. Active macroeconomic policies by government organizations to counter such tendencies became widely accepted.

3. Contemporary mainstream economic theory

The *Keynesian revolution* was short-lived, however. During the second half of the twentieth century, Keynesian ideas were marginalized in favor of more sophisticated versions of the reductionist Walrasian model. This marginalization may have, in part, been driven by misconceptions of how economic system functioned. For example, the period from the end of World War II through the early 1970s, which experienced the fastest ever material economic growth in human history, was seldom interpreted as the success of the active macroeconomic policies carried out by government, but as evidence that the free market system would grow consistently if left alone. Furthermore, economists seemed to recognize the mistake of their pre-Keynesian scientific reductionism by developing mixed macro-micro models that systematically linked the economy's individual consumers, workers, producers, bankers, and investors to the economy's aggregate performance. Macroeconomists referred to this as establishing the *microfoundations* of macroeconomics.

In practice, however, very strong simplifying assumptions were necessary in order to build manageable macroeconomic models that were logically compatible with microeconomic models of individual and firm behavior. As a result, the quest for microfoundations seems to have accomplished little more than to provide logical mathematical justifications for very unrealistic models of individual behavior that could be conveniently linked to equally unrealistic macroeconomic models. Labor markets were most often modeled as competitive markets where labor is paid its marginal product. Real economic phenomena, such as the presence of labor unions, efficiency wages and employers' use of compensation to motivate workers, the fixed costs of hiring and firing workers, the widespread existence of unemployed and underemployed workers in nearly all economies, and the organization of political alliances to deal with such issues, could not be addressed in these models.

Also, all producers were assumed to face rising costs so that the assumption of perfect competition could be sustained in economic models. The high levels of industrial concentration, not to mention the obvious ubiquity of oligopolies and near-monopolies, clearly undermines the legitimacy of models that assume perfect competition. Externalities were assumed away by appealing to a misinterpretation of the *Coase theorem* [Coase, 1960], namely that people, firms, and governments are sufficiently informed and motivated to find ways to negotiate the mutually beneficial sharing of the external costs or benefits. Financial markets were incorporated into neoclassical models by embracing Fama's (1970) convenient model of efficient markets, which assumes all available information is built into asset prices, as well as Friedman's (1953) hypothesis that speculation stabilizes financial markets. Later, Muth's (1960) mathematical definition of rational expectations was built into macroeconomic models by Lucas (1972) to explain why government could not manage an economy in ways to improve economic outcomes. The financial failures that Keynes (1936) linked to financial uncertainty were further pushed out of sight by the theoretical work of Arrow and Debreu (1954) and Debreu (1959), who simply substituted the word *risk* for Keynes' *uncertainty*, defined the former in terms of known probability distributions, and then assumed the existence of a set of competitive markets in *contingent commodities* that enabled all risk to be insured or diversified away. Wrote Debreu (1959, p. 98), presumably seriously: "This new definition of a commodity allows one to obtain a theory of uncertainty free from any probability concept and formally identical with the theory of certainty...." Financial regulation was thus unneceassry, and financial innovations, such as those which sank the global economy in 2008, were positively viewed as adding to contingent markets and, thus, helping to stabilize the economic system.

The reluctance of mainstream economists to embrace the need for more financial regulation and reorganization after the 2008-2009 financial global collapse suggests that they continue to ignore how financial organizations behave and why such behavior causes costly financial collapses, that is, non-linear outcomes. The sharp rise in corporate profits and the increasingly unequal distribution of income that characterizes modern economies such as the U.S. and the U.K. further suggests that economists business organizations are not accurately described under the assumptions of the neoclassical models. For example, mainstream economists often simply assume the special conditions Jensen and Meckling (1976) showed were necessary for managers of private firms to act as faithful servants to the firm's individual stockholders, which include high levels of competition and full information on the part of stockholders. Combined with assumptions of perfect competition and full information, mainstream economists cited Jensen and Meckling to argue that even large corporations would act in ways that promoted the general welfare of society. Clearly, large business organizations can behave in ways that do not reflect the desires and interests of workers, stockholders, or many other groups of people in the economy. Nor can the models that assume competitive and fully-informed markets in which self-interested individuals make fully informed and rational decisions explain the persistent corruption and political activism by business firms, the banding together of workers in labor unions, the demand for collectively provided government services, and the large amounts of money spent by special interest lobbies.

4. Scientific progress

The persistent use of a modeling framework that fails to accurately explain or predict clearly observable economic events flies in the face of science. Economics is not the first science to violate the scientific method, however. In his analysis of the history of science, Thomas Kuhn (1962, p. 2) observed that "science does not tend toward the ideal that our image of its cumulativeness has suggested. Perhaps it is another sort of enterprise." Instead, Kuhn noticed that, throughout human history, small scientific advances often followed systemic cumulative paths, but truly revolutionary scientific changes, which occurred much less often, were usually completely incommensurable with earlier knowledge and lacked even a common standard of measurement. The axioms, or common accepted truths, often differed between major scientific thrusts. Kuhn called revolutionary science a *paradigm shift*, by which he meant a completely new way of observing the world, analyzing evidence, and interpreting conclusions. In economics we often refer to a paradigm as a *school* of thought.

The word *paradigm* is derived from the Greek word *paradeigma*, which means "pattern." The fields of neuroscience, psychology, and behavioral economics, among others, have shown that the human brain is very much aware of patterns, and it tends to try to fit everything it sees into familiar patterns. These patterns, often incorporated into stories, ceremonies, procedures, social organization, and social norms, effectively become part of a group's *culture*. This culture effectively tells practitioners what they should, or should not, study, the types of questions they should seek to answer, and even how they should interpret their findings. Inter-disciplinary research shows that culture tends to be self-reinforcing, which explains why paradigms often persist in the presence of clear anomalies that do not fit the patterns prescribed by the paradigm. The unwarranted persistence of a paradigm becomes even more likely if, as in the case of the field of economics, the group culture discourages economists from explicitly recognizing the presence of a group phenomenon like group culture.

5. The origins of culture

Culture consists of the set of common patterns of human activity and behavior that people value and identify with. More specifically, the United Nations Educational, Scientific and Cultural Organization (UNESCO, 2002) defines culture as follows:

> ...culture should be regarded as the set of distinctive spiritual, material, intellectual and emotional features of society or a social group, and that it encompasses, in addition to art and literature, lifestyles, ways of living together, value systems, traditions, and beliefs.

Culture consists of informal institutions such as traditions, myths, religions, norms of behavior, manners, artistic expressions, and symbols. Culture emerged from the process of human evolution because it enabled humans to cope with the growing complexity of their existence. Fundamentally, culture serves to enhance social cohesion by inducing independently-thinking but socially-inclined individuals to conform to the patterns recognized by others who embrace the same culture. Clearly, when describing the culture of economics, the models that economists commonly use to explain issues and pass along ideas form part of the field's culture.

It is tempting to interpret human development as implying that people have become increasingly capable of engaging in rational thought and functioning without the inherently irrational traditions, habits, and norms that make up culture. A rational individualistic *homo eoconomicus* is an extreme logical conclusion of such an interpretation. Seabright (2010), in fact, highlights humans' ability to engage in abstract thinking as one important reason for humanity's relatively short-term success as a species. But Seabright also points out that humans used their mental capabilities in practical ways that do not match modern economics' definition of rationality because life is much too complex and time-restricted for humans to rationally deliberate their every action. Behavioral economists have suggested that humans follow more realistic strategies. For example, Simon (1955) has used experiments to show that people are likely to take short-cuts and engage in "satisficing, " and Simon (1959) later described people as doing the best they can, but that they are only "boundedly rational" because humans often need to make decisions quickly and without all the facts in hand.

The economic historian and new institutional economist North (2005, pp. 15-16) describes the origins of culture as follows:

> Throughout human history there has always been a large residual that defied rational explanation—a residual to be explained partly by non-rational explanations embodied in witchcraft, magic, religions; but partly by more prosaic non-rational behavior characterized by dogmas, prejudices, "half-baked" theories. Indeed despite the...assertion by eminent theorists that it is not possible to theorize in the face of uncertainty, humans do it all the time; their efforts range from ad hoc assertions and loosely structured beliefs such as those encompassed in the labels "conservative" and "liberal" to elegant systematic ideologies such as Marxism or organized religions.

Keynes (1936) referred to these half-baked theories as "convention," in the sense that, for lack of anything better, some ideas seem to provide a reasonable guide for action, which then becomes the conventional way of doing things. Also, in Chapter 12 of his *General Theory*, Keynes (1936) compared innovators to explorers of the South Pole, who, in a state of uncertainty, drew on their *animal spirits* to decide when to move forward and when to be cautious. Langlois (1986, 1992) refers to North's unproven but convenient ideas as "social rules," and he referred to a group's implicit creation of social institutions as a collective form of "rule making." Social scientists generally consider these "half-baked ideas," "loosely structured beliefs," "conventions," and "social rules" to constitute *culture*.

Neuroscientific research also provides evidence that the human does not function as Muth (1960) hypothesized. Churchland (2002, p. 308) explains the neuroscientific findings precisely as follows:

> The Brain's earliest self-representational capacities arose as evolution found neural network solutions for coordinating and regulating inner-body signals, thereby improving behavioral strategies. Additional flexibility in organizing coherent behavioral options emerges from neura models that represent some of the brain's inner states as states of its body, while representing other signals as perceptions of the external world. Brains manipulate inner models to predict the distinct consequences in the external world of distinct behavioral options.

Using these methods, scientists such as Lebeouf (2002) and Medin and Bazerman (1999), among many other researchers, have confirmed that the automatic and emotional processes in the human brain depend largely on the recognition of patterns. Their experiments show that the human brain becomes agitated when unfamiliar patterns emerge or familiar patterns cannot be found in what is being observed. But it is important to note that, as experiments reported in Frederick (2005) clearly demonstrate, even the most intelligent people routinely misinterpret a problem or an observation because they place it in a familiar pattern that, in fact, does not accurately apply to the problem at hand. By relying in patterns, people often make mistakes.

The human brain thus evolved not only to use abstract reasoning to deal with complex issues, but also to derive practical rules to guide human actions within that complex reality. Quick reactions were required to deal with predators and unexpected natural disasters; long deliberations were not a practical way to deal with the bear that suddenly appeared at the cave entrance.

Humanity did not survive on practical combinations of abstract thinking and clever short-cuts alone, however; humans survived because they also maintained cohesive groups in which members could efficiently interact to generate social outcomes greater than what a simple sum of individual actions could accomplish. The evolution of humans into group animals reflects the safety of numbers, the efficiency of splitting tasks, the benefits of sharing knowledge, and the ability to carry out large projects. By giving shared assertions and mutual beliefs significance, humans were able to suppress some of the independent individual thoughts and actions that would be detrimental to the survival of their social groups. A fundamental purpose of culture, therefore, was to sustain group cohesion in the face of external threats.

In sum, culture enables complex human societies to survive within the constraints of their economic, social, and natural environments. History suggests that human culture does not always achieve the fundamental goal of survival. There have certainly been many conflicts among individuals and between groups of individuals. And, numerous civilizations collapsed because they were not able to deal with all the social and natural challenges they faced. Overall, however, human culture has been quite successful in that it has enabled humans, in a very short evolutionary period of time, to gain a large presence on Earth.

Unfortunately, economists have not done a very good job analyzing the group and organizational behavior that enabled this human evolutionary success. Note that the modern growth theory that has been used extensively to analyze the rapid economic development of the twentieth century is firmly embedded in the neoclassical modeling structure, a structure that effectively denies the development of group phenomena such as culture.

6. Culture and the need for reflexivity

The French sociologist Pierre Bourdieu provides very useful insight into the question of why the neoclassical school and its modeling strategy based on individualism and self-interest persists despite the vast body of real evidence that contradicts its conclusions. Bourdieu is well known for urging his fellow sociologists to actively undertake a systematic and rigorous self-critical analysis of how their own field studies culture. Bourdieu (1977a, 1988, 1989a, 1990, 2005a) referred to such a self-analysis as *reflexivity*.[2] Bourdieu's many years studying how cultures perpetuated unjust and oppressive social structures led him to conclude that sociologists too often let their own culture bias their analysis and interpretations of other cultures. Bourdieu noted that sociologists should know better than anyone how culture distorts perceptions of reality, and he challenged his fellow sociologists to engage in a "sociology of sociology" in order to better understand their own biases. Perhaps economists, too, should follow Bourdieu's suggestion and become more aware of how the culture of their field restricts their analysis. What follows is a brief *sociology of economics* that uses Bourdieu's framework for analyzing culture.

7. The sociology of economics

Bourdieu takes as his starting point the work of the early twentieth century sociologist Max Weber (1978), who recognized that people generally adhere to more than one culture because their position in society often cuts cross traditional concepts of class or culture. Professions like sociology or economics develop strong *subcultures* that are embraced by practitioners that, simultaneously, live in different national and ethnic cultures. This embrace of multiple cultures is important for understanding the widespread acceptance of neoclassical analysis by economists the world over; the economics subculture can apparently survive within many different national and ethnic cultures.

Bourdieu's first analytical concept is the *field*, which he defines as the social or intellectual arena within which people spend much of their day and within which they can best advance their primary economic and social interests. People normally identify with broad national or ethnic cultures, but in going about their daily activities they tend to pay the most attention to their immediate professional or social environments. Many people closely identify themselves with the culture of a particular job, industry, or work environment in which they spend much of their available time and effort. For academics, the term *field* is straightforward because most of an intellectual's life is spent within a well-defined intellectual field. Note, however, that Bourdieu's concept of a field is more general. For example, teenagers tend to embrace the culture of their school environment and the new social relationships that they develop there. Members of the military adopt a distinctive military culture of hierarchy, obedience, and violence. And, athletes focus on a

---

[2] See also the discussions on reflexivity in Wacquant (1989) and Bourdieu and Wacquant (1992).

culture likely to include specific rules, norms, and perspectives on repetitive training, physical prowess, competition, and, depending on the sport, aggressive behavior.

Each individual usually spends a large proportion of time focused on the one *field* because that is where they judge their success in life. For example, a teenager may clash with the culture of his/her household or even that of his/her nation, but showing up in school wearing clothes that clash with the school culture would be unthinkable! Similarly, economists come from a great many ethnic, national, and other social cultures, but as quickly becomes obvious to anyone attending an international economics conference, they all dress, act, talk, and present research that uses very similar models, procedures, and presentations. Nearly all economists tend to judge their colleagues by the same set of criteria covering the subjects, methods, and procedures that have come to be viewed as appropriate in their field.

Bourdieu develops two useful concepts that help to more precisely describe the *culture* of a field. First, people in a field adopt certain attitudes, behaviors, and dispositions, which Bourdieu defines as the field's *habitus*, a term he took from the writings of Aristotle and Max Weber. A habitus is a set of *subjective* but persistent perceptions, customs, conventions, norms, mannerisms, behaviors, expressions, and procedures that are deemed appropriate or "normal" by practitioners in the field. Habitus effectively constitutes both a person's personal disposition towards others and the set of behaviors by which she thinks others within the field will judge her to be one of them. Bourdieu effectively straddles the long-running sociological debate between subjectivity and objectivity by defining the field as objective and the habitus as subjective. Bourdieu argued that people develop the *subjective* dispositions and attitudes of their habitus in order to be successful in their well-defined *objective* field.

A soldier, therefore, is likely to adopt a habitus characterized by a clear willingness to engage in aggressive behavior, an unquestioning acceptance of authority and rank, as well as a strong affirmation of group loyalty. A businessperson's habitus tends to be characterized by an admiration for aggressive salesmanship, a disdain for government restrictions on business activity, and a positive response to monetary rewards. An economist's habitus most likely includes the use of neoclassical models to analyze a set of issues from the perspective of a market economy, a preference for mathematics in stating hypotheses, familiarity with statistical methods, and a reluctance to address issues that extend beyond the market economy or, heaven forbid, into other disciplines. Recall our general discussion of culture and group behavior; venturing into other disciplines tends to be viewed as disloyalty to one's own culture, and such disloyalty could weaken the cohesion of the group. Hence, outside ideas are instinctively mocked, but the models and methods that fit the neoclassical framework of the habitus are seldom criticized from within the field.

Bourdieu points out that there is an inherent conflict between the reality of one's field and the arbitrary nature of much of what comprises the field's habitus. Psychologically, it is difficult for an intelligent person to deal with this combination of an *objective* field and a *subjective* habitus. Therefore, human societies, groups and organizations within human societies, and fields develop, largely unconsciously, sets of beliefs, symbols, and popular stories that provide some justification for the subjective and somewhat arbitrary habitus associated with one's objective field. Bourdieu calls these sets of well-established but largely unproven beliefs, stories, and philosophies *doxa*. These doxa include unproven but widely accepted religious dogma, general social philosophies, and assorted political views. Doxa provide the broad patterns with which people judge their behavior in their field, and the behavior of others within their field and elsewhere.

A field's doxa includes those "half-baked ideas" that North (2005) argued were social constructs that enabled people and societies to deal with the poorly understood complexities that they routinely faced. Together, the habitus and its supporting doxa constitute what we call *culture*.

Arguably, the doxa that underlies the habitus of economics is the so-called *neoliberal* doctrine. As described in detail by Harvey (2005), this is a set of beliefs that include the characterization of individual humans as always rational and scientifically objective in their decision making.[3] Neoliberalism also includes the belief that "an economy" can be reasonably modeled as a system of competitive markets in which the "invisible hand" does a reasonable job of transforming self-interested individual behavior into an optimal state of general well-being. Neoliberal thinkers argue that free markets are fundamental to the important social goal of giving individuals their "freedom to choose." Markets are believed to offer greater freedom and better options than "coerced" government programs and regulatory regimes. Neoliberalism also has a strong bias against collective action and a strong bias in favor of private enterprise. Finally, the doxa of economics places the welfare of the individual front and center, to the point of suggesting that any form of collective action must necessarily be coerced and thus necessarily welfare reducing.

---

[3] Bourdieu (2005b) and Wacquant (2009) explicitly describe the doxa of economics as consisting of neoliberal ideas.

The policies imposed on many indebted developing economies by the International Monetary Fund after the 1982 global debt crisis, the so-called *Washington Consensus* policies, were a direct reflection of this neo-liberal doxa. These policies included free trade, privatization of government assets, conservative monetary policies to reduce inflation, balanced government budgets, the elimination of labor market regulations, and diminished financial market regulation. The austerity policies currently being imposed in indebted countries of the European Union, such as Greece and Ireland, are another reflection of the Washington consensus and its underlying neoliberal doxa. It is still not clear that these policies have actually improved human well-being anywhere, but they have nevertheless been given very favorable treatment in economic textbooks and most research without causing much debate among mainstream economists. Of course, it is not the function of a doxa to generate debate; the doxa must have widespread and unquestioned acceptance if it is to serve its function of mitigating the urge for economists to question the arbitrariness of the methods and policy options that are in economists' habitus.

The neoliberal doxa of free markets and individualism closely reflects many fundamental aspects of the broader Western social culture, especially that of the United States, the United Kingdom, and other countries with strong Anglo-Saxon cultural heritage. Economists, by projecting their subculture into the rest of the world, are, therefore, effectively forcing major elements of Western culture on others in the guise of science. Third world economists trained at Western universities or taught from Western economics textbooks effectively serve as the foot soldiers for Western culture in their native countries. Respected Western economists use neoclassical models to judge economies and economic policies everywhere in the world. In short, most economists behave like the Western sociologists Bourdieu criticized for judging foreign cultures from the perspective of their own Western cultures.

The obvious example of bias in the subject matter of economics is the tendency for economists to focus exclusively on market activities, to use data generated by markets, and to interpret the observed results as if all economic activity was undertaken by rational individuals operating in competitive markets. Recall the quote by Bourdieu at the start of this article. Hence, most economic research analyzes activities included in measured GDP, uses market prices and quantities to quantify human economic activity, and even uses market generated prices to proxy for the value non-market activity if such activity is included in the analysis. Of course, most non-market activity, such as household production and volunteer work, is effectively ignored and given the implicit value of zero.[4] Any objective examination of real world economic activity shows that most human economic interactions do not occur among individuals in formal markets, but among people interacting in a great variety of non-market settings, including within households, within business organizations, in voluntary interactions, in government, and in various collective activities.

At the same time, the neoliberal doxa of economics leads most economists to view issues such as psychological happiness, environmental problems, and species losses in the natural environment as *non-economic issues* that fall outside the field of economics. The narrow scope of most professional economics journals reflects the conformity of the economics habitus to the neoliberal doxa that closely equates economic activity with market activity.

A most important aspect of the culture of economics is that it discourages economists from studying group behavior and the role of organizations in human societies. Therefore, despite overwhelming evidence to the contrary from numerous fields of science and social science, mainstream economists still almost exclusively use welfare functions that aggregate the individual welfare of separable individuals. Even after giving Nobel prizes to behavioral economists, for example Kahnemann, Tversky, and Akerlof, for studying the psychological aspects of economic activity, and organizational economists such as Ostrom and Williamson for studying organizational aspects of economic activity, most economists continue to measure economic growth in terms of individuals interacting in markets. They thus pay relatively little attention to the role of groups and organizations, such as labor unions, large corporations, and large financial firms, in explaining economic outcomes. The power of culture is strong.

8. Symbolic violence

In fact, culture is not only a reflection of the dominant paradigm, it also tends to actively protect that paradigm from rivals that seek a paradigm shift. Bourdieu (1986, 1989b) explains that culture has staying power because it exploits people's inherent desire to maintain acceptance within the group. People tend to consciously or unconsciously interpret reality in ways that often effectively leads them to act against their own individual

---

[4] For example, feminist economists, such as Waring (1988), Benería (1992), Himmelweit (1995), Folbre (1996, 2006), have criticized mainstream economics for ignoring household activity as a major contributor to economic production, and they estimated the value of such non-market activity to be on the order of measured GDP.

interests because they also value social approval, friendship, and a role in their society and field. Recall that the evolutionary role of culture was, at least in part, to enable individual behavior that benefits the welfare of the whole group, not necessarily each individual. Culture can, in numerous cases, be oppressive.

In much of his research, Bourdieu (1986, 1989a) focused on cultural oppression. One of his themes was that such oppression was driven by an unequal distribution of *cultural capital*. Bourdieu's use of the word *capital* to describe a person's familiarity with, and ease of acting within, a culture reflects the accumulation of human culture through the long, slow processes of education, social experience, family upbringing, assimilation, and learning.

Bourdieu described various forms of cultural capital. For example, *inherited cultural capital* includes learned behaviors such as knowledge, habits, language and dialect, social mannerisms, and conversational manners. Economists definitely acquire a distinctive jargon and knowledge. There is also *objectified cultural capital*, which includes real physical things such as a musical instrument, a carpenter's tool box, or, in the case of economists, an office computer and shelves of books and professional journals. In each case, the musician, the carpenter, and the economists would lose status if they did not possess such objectified capital. Note that the size of the collection of professional journals clearly reflects an economist's tenure in the profession. Finally, *institutionalized cultural capital* includes diplomas, awards, certifications, and other official credentials, whose accumulation also takes a lengthy effort. Together, these forms of cultural capital give those who possess more cultural capital power over those who possess less.

The use of this power to impose one's will over another person with less cultural capital is referred to by Bourdieu (1977b, 1986, 1989b, 2001) as *symbolic violence*. Discrimination and harassment are overt forms of symbolic violence. But there are also many subtle forms of symbolic violence, such as a frown or look of disapproval by a parent that makes a child change its behavior or the concerned mention of "unfinished work" by a boss that effectively signals to an employee that (s)he had better put in some extra hours over the weekend. Symbolic violence among adults is fundamental to the perpetuation of gender, ethnic, and age inequalities. Bourdieu (2001) shows that symbolic violence often leads people to accept what are, objectively viewed, injustices because they adjust their doxa to match the social field they inhabit. He documents how working class children often accept the social order as legitimate and thus view the educational success of their upper- and middle-class peers as a reflection of the latter's greater ability or harder work rather than the social privilege that enabled them to acquire the mannerisms, accent, and clothing associated with the habitus of a higher class.

Economics graduates of lower-rated universities, say the University of Nebraska, see the professional success of the graduates of higher-ranked universities, such as Harvard, MIT, or UC Berkeley, as a legitimate reflection of the latter's greater ability or their harder work, even though in reality the institutionalized cultural capital (the diplomas) are seldom more than the result of class-based inherited cultural and economic capital. Economic pressures, such as the need for income or an employer's health insurance, often lead a worker to accept the underlying doxa of hierarchy and the acceptance of the existing distribution of economic and cultural capital that justifies the unequal economic outcomes. So economics PhDs from Nebraska accept one-year instructor contracts at lower level universities while the Harvard graduates get the tenure track positions at the higher ranked universities. According to Bourdieu (2001), people are complicit in the symbolic violence they experience because they subconsciously adjust their doxa in order to maintain their sense of dignity within what they are forced to accept as the immutable reality of the social or professional field they inhabit. The resignation to the existing social order is due, according to Bourdieu, to the fact that redistributing cultural capital in order to reduce symbolic violence is likely to be a gradual, difficult, and slow process, and those who have the most cultural capital are likely to use it to resist redistributive measures.

A paradigm shift constitutes a shift in cultural capital. By intimidating actual and potential purveyors of alternative paradigms, those with the greatest investments in the current paradigm use symbolic violence that effectively protects both the doxa and habitus from contradictory facts, or what Thomas Kuhn (1962) called *anomalies*. If anomalies are openly and objectively discussed and examined, a paradigm shift becomes more likely. But within the strong culture of economics, few economists will question their neoclassical models much less their neoliberal doxa. They received strong and continuous approval for mastering neoclassical economics from their professors during graduate school, and after graduation they continue to receive implicit reassurance of the legitimacy of the doxa and habitus from colleagues, journal editors, and employers. As an illustration of the subtle nature of symbolic violence, consider, say, a Marxist economist in line for promotion and in need of increasing her publication record to justify the promotion; she might very well convince herself that it is permissible for a Marxist to write an article based on a standard neoclassical model that reflects an idealized capitalist economic structure because such an article would be more likely to get published in a "first-tier" economics journal. A further justification would be that unless she gains the promotion, she will not be able to do good Marxist economic analysis in the future. In the meantime, of course, the dominant paradigm is not challenged.

In many intellectual fields like economics, the symbolic violence is most often carried out by the field's most highly regarded members who serve on the editorial boards of professional journals and the faculty committees that hire, promote, and fire new faculty members. Thus, a young assistant professor seeking to publish and gain tenure will be "well-advised" by her older mentors to write articles that apply only neoclassical analysis. Course content in the leading economics departments, dissertation advice, and the selection criteria for research grants further install the orthodox habitus and doxa in the minds of the young students who will become our future economists. Outside of academia, the corporate-funded think tanks, the Federal Reserve Bank in the U.S. and other central banks elsewhere, international agencies such as the IMF, World Bank, and OECD, the business press, and private financial firms also keep the neoclassical models and other elements of the economics habitus firmly entrenched by means of their employment practices, their ability to influence policy and the press, and their money that funds research, publication, grants, internships, and philanthropy.

9. A case for pluralism?

The above sociological examination of the culture of economics suggests that, in order to more effectively study organizations and alternative forms of economic behavior, economists must find a way to free themselves from the constraints imposed by the field's present culture. The culture of economics must change, both its neoliberal doxa and its associated neoclassical habitus. As already stated, the doxa of individualism and free choice, which supports the aggregate welfare functions that are so well established in the habitus, is not only technically problematic for the analysis of organizations or group behavior, but that same doxa, and the habitus it supports, intimidate economists to avoid such analysis altogether. Economists must first find ways to overcome the symbolic violence emanating from the field's dominant neoclassical/neoliberal culture.

Any brief examination of the history of economic thought, as in section 2 above, shows that there are, in fact, many alternative approaches to economics that could prove useful for understanding our complex economic existence. Some of the alternative paradigms readily available to economists willing to look outside the culture of the mainstream would extend economic analysis beyond the confines of a market economy, and others would encourage more holistic approaches that incorporate the complex ties of the economy to the social and natural spheres of human existence. Some economists already operate successfully outside the neoclassical constraints on economic thought and research. For example, behavioral economists combine psychology and economics in order to analyze economic issues with much more realistic models of human behavior and more complete measures of human welfare. Ecologists and environmental economists are addressing the environmental externalities that neoclassical economists have largely ignored. Political scientists and political economists provide valuable insight into the causes and effects of economic policies. As already noted, feminist economists have investigated household activity and gender in the workplace to counter so much of the mainstream analysis that focuses on market activities and treats workers as homogeneous or "representative" individuals devoid of gender, age, class, culture, or other historical characteristics. Recent Nobel laureates Ostrom (2005, 2009) and Williamson (1975, 2002) have moved beyond the neoclassical individual *homo oeconomicus* to actively study business organizations, group outcomes, and alternative ways in which societies can undertake collective economic actions. Institutional economists have studied groups, classes, and economic power since the nineteenth century, as have Marxist economists.

One strategy for achieving paradigmatic freedom, therefore, is to begin reducing the symbolic violence against those who advocate for alternative paradigms. Academia and other economic research organizations could eliminate their discrimination against practitioners who do not share the majority's doxa and habitus. Another strategy that has been used with some success is to establish alternative think tanks; the New Economics Foundation, the Levy Institute, and the Economic Policy Institute are examples of research institutes that are willing to address issues outside the dominant economics culture. Better yet, the economics profession could actively pursue pluralism and maintain many alternative paradigms in the habitus of economics. The establishment of paradigmatic multi-culturalism in the field of economics would not only enable new paradigms to get a fair hearing, but, as Weehuizen (2007) points out, it would prevent some new paradigm and its doxa and habitus from oppressing future revolutionaries.

10. Symbolic violence is backed by economic power

Efforts to incorporate paradigmatic pluralism into the field of economics have been extremely difficult, however. As noted, the present culture of economics is strong. But something else is at work to prevent the emergence of alternative economic paradigms: powerful economic interests have been increasingly able to use the political power structure to support the dominant neoliberal/neoclassical paradigm. Reflexive economists must, therefore, deal with more than just the culture of their field.

It is interesting to note that the revolutionary Keynes (1936, p. viii) recognized the power of culture, as evidenced in the preface to his *General Theory of Employment, Interest, and Money*:

> The composition of this book has been for the author a long struggle of escape, and so must the reading of it be for most readers if the author's assault upon them is to be successful,–a struggle of escape from habitual modes of thought and expression. The ideas which are here expressed so laboriously are extremely simple and should be obvious. The difficulty lies, not in the new ideas, but in escaping from the old ones, which ramify, for those of us brought up as most of us have been, into every corner of our minds.

But Keynes underestimated the strength of the active opposition to his ideas by business and financial interests.

Indeed, his new ideas were almost immediately watered down to reduce their clash with the prevailing economics culture, as evidenced by the work of other prominent mainstream economists such as Hicks (1939) and Samuelson (1948). The intellectual rejection of Keynesian ideas was actively stoked by business and financial interests opposed to the policies, such as Roosevelt's *New Deal*, that the Keynesian paradigm called for. For example, Colander and Landreth (1996) describe how, prior to the appearance of Samuelson's (1948) commercially successful textbook with its illogical combination of a watered-down Keynesian macroecnomic model with traditional neoclassical microeconomic models, an authentically Keynesian textbook by Tarshis (1947) was driven out of U.S. universities by a business-supported campaign directed at university administrators and trustees. Keynesianism was also abandoned by politicians who found themselves under pressure from conservative business and financial interests. For example, in 1937 President Roosevelt reversed some of his stimulative macroeconomic policies at the behest of financial and business leaders despite accurate warnings from his own economists that this would push the economy back into recession.

All in all, by the 1970s Keynes' ideas had been marginalized and the neoclassical ideas were firmly back in the habitus of the field of economics.

Today, wealthy individuals and well-organized business and financial groups exercise their power by means of costly public relations, advertising, and lobbying activities. By "investing" in the promotion of their interests, private financial interests have largely captured the major political parties in most democratic countries as well as the news media that communicate political events and debates to the public. When the news media seek economists to provide commentary and insight into economic issues, more often than not they interview economists who work for business or financial firms, not independent universities or impartial research organizations. These business and financial economists almost always echo the themes of free markets, deregulation, and further privatization, as if the neoclassical paradigm of rational individuals operating in perfectly competitive markets represents our economic reality.

11. Conclusions and comments

With the neoliberal doxa firmly in place, economists maintain the rational individual *homo eoconomicus* at the center of their economic analysis. This means economists have less motivation to engage in research, writing, or teaching that would reveal the power of organizations and other forms of group behavior. In short, powerful lobbying and advocacy organizations work closely together on behalf of private business and financial organizations to actively support a group culture in the organized field of economics that effectively discourages its practitioners from studying those very same organizations and forms of group and social behavior. The transnational corporations and financial conglomerates that dominate the global economy thus often fly under the misdirected radar of mainstream economics.

This conclusion reminds us of the words of Robert Heilbroner, who many years ago noted that "[t]he best kept secret in economics is that economics is about the study of capitalism."[5] After focusing on the culture of economics, however, it is clear that we have to slightly revise Heilbroner's conclusion: economics is, in fact, about the study of a *mythical market system* that actually has little resemblance to the real global capitalist system we live in today. That is not to say that mainstream economics is irrelevant, however. From within that quaint mythical world economists generate very useful

---

[5] Quoted in Palley (1998), p. 15.

intellectual support for the neoliberal policy agenda that favors the business and financial organizations that have come to dominate the real monopolized and financialized economic system. Mainstream economists therefore enjoy a fairly comfortable life. And, they enjoy that life free of any feelings of guilt because their quaint culture also assures them that the economics they do is all about the maximization of human welfare.

References

Arrow, K. And Debreu, G. (1954) Existence of an Equilibrium for a Competitive Economy. *Econometrica*, 22, pp. 265-290.

Benería, L. (1992) Accounting for Women's Work: The Progress of Two Decades. *World Development*, 20(11), pp. 1547-1460.

Bourdieu, P. (1977a) *Outline of a theory of practice*. Cambridge: Cambridge University Press.

Bourdieu, P. (1977b) Symbolic Power. In: GLEESON, D (ed.) *Identity and structure*, Driffield: Nafferton Books.

Bourdieu, P. (1986) The Forms of Capital. In: RICHARDSON, J. G. (ed.) *Handbook of theory and research for the sociology of education*. New York: Greenwood Press.

Bourdieu, P. (1988) *Homo academicus*. Cambridge: Polity Press.

Bourdieu, P. (1989a) *La noblesse d'etat: grands corps et grands écoles*. Paris: Editions de Mimuit.

Bourdieu, P. (1989b) Social Space and Symbolic Power. *Sociological Theory* 7(1), pp. 14-25.

Bourdieu, P. (1990) *In other words: essays toward a reflexive sociology*. Stanford: Stanford University Press.

Bourdieu, P. (2001) *Masculine domination*. Cambridge: Polity Press.

Bourdieu, P. (2005a) *Science of science and reflexivity*. Chicago: University of Chicago Press.

Bourdieu, P. (2005b) *The social structures of the economy*. Cambridge, U.K.: Polity Press.

Bourdieu, P. And Wacquant, L. (1992) *An invitation to reflexive sociology*. Chicago: University of Chicago Press.

Churchland, P.S. (2002) Self-Representation in Nervous Systems. *Science*, 296(April 12), pp. 308-310.

Coase, R. (1960) The Problem of Social Costs. *The Journal of Law and Economics*, 3(1), pp. 1-44.

Colander, D. And Landreth, H. (1996) *The coming of Keynesianism to America*. Brookfield, Vermont: Edward Elgar.

Debreu, G. (1959) *Theory of value*. New Haven, CN: Yale University Press.

Fama, E. (1970), Efficient Capital Markets: A Review of Theory and Empirical Work. *Journal of Finance*, 25(3), pp. 383-417.

Folbre, N. (1994). Children as Public Goods. *American Economic Review*, 84(2), pp. 86-90.

Folbre, N. (2006) Measuring Care: Gender, Empowerment, and the Care Economy. *Journal of Human Development*, 7(2), pp. 183--99.

Frederick, S. (2005) Cognitive Reflection and Decision Making. *Journal of Economic Perspectives*, 19(4), pp. 25-42.

Friedman, M. (1953) The Case for Flexible Exchange Rates. In: FRIEDMAN, M. (ed.). *Essays on positive economics*. Chicago: University of Chicago Press, pp. 157-203.

Harvey, D. (2005) *A brief history of neoliberalism*. New York: Oxford University Press.

Hicks, J.R. (1937) Mr Keynes and the classics. *Econometrica*, 5(2), pp. 147–159.

Himmelweit, S. (1995) The Discovery of "Unpaid Work": The Social Consequences of the Expansion of Work. *Feminist Economics*, 1(2), pp. 1--19.

Jensen, M. and Meckling, W. (1976) Theory of the Firm: Managerial Behavior, Agency Costs and Ownership Structure. *Journal of Financial Economics*, 3(4), pp. 305–60.

Keynes, J.M. (1936[1964]) *The general theory of employment, interest, and money*. New York: Harcourt Brace Jovanovich.

Kuhn, T. (1962) *The structure of scientific revolutions*. Chicago: University of Chicago Press.

Langlois, R. (1986) Coherence and Flexibility: Social Institutions in a World of Radical Uncertainty. In: Kirzer, I. (ed.). *Subjectivism, intelligibility, and economic understanding: essays in honor of the eightieth birthday of Ludwig Lachmann*. New York: New York University Press, pp. 171-191.

Langlois, R. (1992) Orders and Organizations: Toward an Austrian Theory of Social Institutions. In: caldwell, B. and Böhm, S. (eds.). *Austrian economics: tensions and new directions*. Dordrecht: Kluwer Academic Publishers.

Leboeuf, R.A. (2002) Alternating Selves and Conflicting Choices: Identity Salience and Preference Inconsistency. *Dissertation Abstracts International*, 63(2-B), p. 1088.

Lucas, R.E. (1972) Expectations and the Neutrality of Money. *Journal of Economic Theory*, 4(1), pp. 103-124.

Marshall, A. (1920 [1959]) *Principles of economics*. 8th ed. London: MacMillan.

Medin, D. and Bazerman, M. (1999) Broadening Behavioral Decision Research: Multiple Levels of Cognitive Processing. *Psychonomic Bulletin and Review*, 6(4), pp. 533-47.

Muth, J.F. (1961) Rational Expectations and the Theory of Price Movements. *Econometrica*, 29, pp. 315-335.

North, D.C. (2005) *Understanding the process of economic change*. Princeton, NJ: Princeton University Press.

Ostrom, E. (2005) *Understanding institutional diversity*, Princeton, NJ: Princeton University Press.

Ostrom, E. (2009) A General Framework for Analyzing Sustainability of Social-Ecological Systems. *Science*, 325(5939), pp. 419-422.

Palley, T. (1998) *Plenty of nothing: the downsizing of the American dream and the case for structural Keynesianism.* Princeton: Princeton University Press.

Samuelson, P. (1948) *Economics.* New York: McGraw-Hill.

Seabright, P. (2010) *The company of strangers: a natural history of economic life.* 2nd Ed. Princeton, NJ: Princeton University Press.

Simon, H. (1955) A Behavioral Model of Rational Choice," *Quarterly Journal of Economics.* 69, pp. 99-118.

Simon, H. (1959) Theories of Decision-Making in Economics and Behavioral Science. *American Economic Review*, 49, pp. 253-283.

Smith, A. (1776 [1976]) *An inquiry into the nature and causes of the wealth of nations.* Chicago: University of Chicago Press.

Tarshis, L. (1947) *The elements of economics.* Boston: Houghton Mifflin.

UNESCO (2002) Universal Declaration of Cultural Diversity. Available from: www.unesco.org [Accessed 04.10.13]

Wacquant, L. (1989) Toward a Reflexive Sociology: A Workshop with Pierre Bourdieu. *Sociological Theory*, 7(1), pp. 26-63.

Wacquant, L. (2009) *Punishing the poor: the neoliberal government of social insecurity.* Durham, NC: Duke University Press.

Walras, L. (1874) *Éléments d'économie politique pure, ou théorie de la richesse sociale*

Waring, M. (1988) *If women counted: a new feminist economics.* San Francisco: Harper & Row.

Weber, M. (1978) *Economy and society*, Berkeley: University of California Press.

Weehuizen, R. (2007) Interdisciplinary and Problem-Based Learning in Economics Education: The Case of Infonomics. In: Groenewegen, J. (ed.) *Teaching pluralism in economics.* Northampton, MA: Edward Elgar, pp. 155-188.

Williamson, O. (1975) *Markets and hierarchies: analysis and anti-trust implications.* New York: Free Press.

Williamson, O. (2002) The Theory of the Firm as Governance Structure: From Choice to Contract. *Journal of Economic Perspectives*, 16(3), pp. 171-195.

Weak Expansions: A Distinctive Feature of the Business Cycle in Latin America and the Caribbean

Esteban Pérez Caldentey, Daniel Titelman and Pablo Carvallo[1]
Economic Commission for Latin America and the Caribbean
Financing for Development Division

Abstract

Using two standard cycle methodologies (Classical and Deviation Cycle) and a comprehensive sample of 83 countries worldwide, including all developing regions, we show that the Latin American and Caribbean (LAC) cycle exhibits two distinctive features. First, and most importantly, its expansion performance is shorter and for the most part less intense than that of the rest of the regions considered, and in particular than that of East Asia and the Pacific. East Asia and the Pacific's expansions last five years longer than those of LAC, and its output gain is 50% greater than that of LAC. Second, LAC tends to exhibit contractions that are not significantly different in terms of duration and amplitude than those of other regions. Both these features imply that the complete Latin American and Caribbean cycle has, overall, the shortest duration and smallest amplitude in relation to other regions. The specificities of the Latin American and Caribbean cycle are not confined to the short run. These are also reflected in variables such as productivity and investment, which are linked to long-run growth. East Asia and the Pacific's cumulative gain in labor productivity during the expansionary phase is twice that of LAC. Moreover, the evidence also shows that the effects of the contraction in public investment surpass those of the expansion leading to a declining trend over the entire cycle. In this sense we suggest that policy analysis needs to increase its focus on the expansionary phase of the cycle. Improving our knowledge of the differences in the expansionary dynamics of countries and regions, can further our understanding of the differences in their rates of growth and levels of development. We also suggest that while, the management of the cycle affects the short-run fluctuations of economic activity and hence volatility, it is not trend neutral. Hence, the effects of aggregate demand management policies may be more persistent over time and less transitory than currently thought.

Keywords: Latin American business cycle, classical cycle, deviation cycle, expansions, trend and cycle, productivity, investment

JEL Classifications: E32, O11, O54, F44

[1] The opinions here expressed are the authors' own and may not coincide with those of the Economic Commission for Latin America and the Caribbean (ECLAC). An earlier version of this paper was presented at the ECLAC workshop, "Policies for Sustained Growth with Equality" (October 29–30, 2012, Santiago, Chile). We wish to thank the participants for the useful comments received during the presentation and discussion of the paper and in particular to Cecilia Vera for very valuable suggestions for improving the arguments and coherence of the paper. We are also grateful to John Rand and Finn Tarp (University of Copenhagen) for sharing the computer codes for the Bry-Boschan algorithm procedure in Mat Lab.

Introduction

In this paper, we use the "Classical Cycle" and "Deviation Cycle" standard methodologies to characterize the business cycle for Latin American and the Caribbean in relation to that of other regions of the world, placing the focus of the comparison on East Asia and the Pacific. We characterize the complete cycle and its phases (contraction/expansion) in terms of duration and amplitude for a sample of 83 countries, 44 of which belong to the different developing regions of the world and 39 of which are classified as high income economies.[2] The analysis is undertaken using quarterly data covering the period 1989–2012.[3]

The majority of the results obtained are robust to the use of both the "Classical Cycle" and "Deviation Cycle" methodologies. These show that the Latin American and Caribbean cycle displays two distinct features. On the one hand, and most importantly, the Latin American and Caribbean region has weaker expansions relative to other regions of the world. On the other hand, Latin America and the Caribbean have contractions whose duration and amplitude do not differ significantly from those of other developing countries. As a result, the full cycle of expansions and contractions exhibits, on a general basis, the shortest duration and smallest amplitude among all regions.

The dynamics of the Latin American and Caribbean cycle are not confined exclusively to short-run analysis. These are also reflected in the behavior of variables such as productivity and investment, which are generally identified as determinants of long-run growth.

In particular, the tenuous nature of the expansionary phase of the cycle is reflected in the fact that productivity growth in Latin America and the Caribbean during that cycle phase tends to be below that of other developing regions, notably East Asia and the Pacific. Moreover, the evidence suggests that, as a general rule, the growth of public capital formation during the expansion is unable to supersede its contraction in the downward phase of the cycle, leading to a decline in the level of public investment during the complete business cycle.

The paper is divided into six sections. The first underscores the importance of studying cyclical behavior, especially in the case of Latin America and the Caribbean. The second section briefly explains the methodologies and describes the dataset used in the

---

[2] In our categorization of developing economies we include low and middle income economies following the World Bank Classification.
[3] Data for the period 1980 to 2012 was not available for all the countries included in our study. See the annex for the countries included and time period covered.

paper. The third, fourth, and fifth sections concentrate on the stylized facts of the Latin American and Caribbean cycle. The sixth section discusses, albeit in a preliminary fashion, the linkages between the cycle and long-run outcomes. The last section concludes with a reflection on cycle analysis and pinpoints directions for further research on the topic.

1. Why we should not give short shrift to the cycle

Over the past three decades, the performance of Latin America and the Caribbean region has been characterized by an increasing degree of volatility in terms of output and investment behavior (among other variables). Moreover, volatility in Latin America and the Caribbean has tended to surpass that of other regions of the world (Titelman, Pérez Caldentey, and Minzer 2008; Calderón and Fuentes 2012; ECLAC 2002, 2012).

At the same time, Latin America and the Caribbean have experienced lower long-run growth in relation to other regions. Table 1 shows the evolution of GDP per capita growth for Latin America and the Caribbean, the Organisation for Economic Co-operation and Development (OECD) member states (high income economies), and selected developing regions of the world for the period 1970–2011.

The evidence indicates that Latin America and the Caribbean had the highest levels of GDP per capita growth in the 1970s in relation to other regions, with the exception of East Asia and the Pacific. Thereafter, the region has registered one of the lowest rates of growth of GDP per capita in relation to other developing regions for most of the periods under consideration (1981–1990, 1991–2000, 2001–2009, and 2001–2011). Moreover, the growth differential between Latin America and the Caribbean and other regions (such as the case of East Asia and the Pacific) has widened over time (see Table 1).

The most recent period of expansion (2003–2007) does not constitute an exception to this observed trend. During this time, Latin America and the Caribbean experienced the highest average rate of growth in over three decades. The regional average per capita growth rate reached 3.7 percent, surpassing not only that of the 1980s lost decade and that registered during the free market structural reform era (1991–2000; 1.4 percent), but also that of the 1970s (3.2 percent).

Table 1 GDP per capita growth by region/income grouping, 1971–2011

	East Asia & Pacific	Europe & Central Asia	High income: OECD	Latin America & Caribbean	Middle East & North Africa	South Asia	Sub-Saharan Africa
1971–1980	4.5	...	2.7	3.2	2.7	0.7	0.9
1981–1990	5.7	-1.7	2.7	-0.8	0.2	3.0	-0.9
1991–2000	7.1	-1.7	1.9	1.6	1.8	3.2	-0.3
2003–2007	**9.3**	**7.4**	**1.9**	**3.7**	**3.3**	**6.6**	**3.0**
2001–2011	8.2	4.7	0.9	2.2	2.6	5.3	2.1

Source: World Development Indicators and Global Finance, World Bank (2012)

However, on a comparative basis, Latin America and the Caribbean's performance was by no means an exceptional one. In fact, the regional rate of growth remained significantly below those of East Asia and the Pacific (9.3 percent), Europe and Central Asia (7.4 percent), and South Asia (6.6 percent).

Part of the explanation of both the high degree of volatility and low level of long-run growth lies in the specific features of the Latin American and Caribbean cycle.

Cycle fluctuations and their characteristics define the pattern and nature of volatility. Moreover, in spite of the fact that cycle fluctuations are traditionally associated with a short-period context, these can also impinge on long-run growth by their effects on investment and productivity, among other variables. In this regard, the cycle itself as well as the policies designed and implemented to confront and manage its fluctuations is not trend-neutral. From here follows the importance of analyzing, characterizing,, and identifying the distinguishing features of the Latin American and Caribbean cycle in relation to other developing regions. In the sections that follow, we place particular focus on the comparison with East Asia and the Pacific, which is often used for this region as a benchmark for assessing social and economic progress and development.

2. The methodological approach

Business cycles are generally defined as periodic patterns in the fluctuations of macroeconomic variables including output, unemployment, consumption, investment, and prices over months or years.[4] In this sense, the cycle can be viewed as a series of turning points (peaks and troughs) with alternating phases of expansion and contraction.

Currently there are two main approaches to the analysis of the business cycle, the Classical Cycle and Deviation Cycle.[5] The former defines the cycle as a series of turning points in the level of real aggregate economic activity. For the latter, the cycle is defined in terms of the deviations of real aggregate economic activity from its trend (or potential output). Both methodologies can be used to characterize the cycle in terms of duration and intensity. However, due to methodological differences, the Deviation Cycle produces longer contractions than the Classical Cycle and fails to capture the asymmetry of the cycle.[6]

In this paper, we use both methodologies to show that our results are not dependent on any given approach. Moreover, to further strengthen our arguments, both methodologies are applied on a comprehensive dataset comprising 83 economies worldwide and including all developing regions.

---

[4] The standard definition is provided in the classical text by Burns and Mitchell (1946, p. 3): "Business Cycles are a type of fluctuation found in the aggregate economic activity of nations that organize their work mainly in business enterprises: a cycle consists of expansions occurring at about the same time in many economic activities, followed by similarly general recessions, and revivals which merge into the expansion phase of the next cycle; this sequence of changes is recurrent but not periodic; *in duration business cycles vary from more than one year to ten to twelve years; they are not divisible into shorter* cycles of similar character with amplitudes approximating their own." See Medio (2008) for a review of business cycle theories.

[5] Other approaches include the rocking horse view championed by Ragnar Frisch and the growth rate cycle. Frisch's approach built on Knut Wicksell's and distinguished between the propagation and the impulse problem. As he put it: "There need not be any synchronism between the initiating force or forces and the movement of the swinging system. This fact has frequently been overlooked in economic cycle analysis. If a cyclical variation is analyzed from the point of view of a free oscillation, we have to distinguish between two fundamental problems: first, the propagation problem; second the impulse problem" (Frisch 1933, p. 171). See Pagan (2003) and Zambelli (1997) for a critique. The growth refers to fluctuations in the growth rate of economic activity. Within this approach, an expansion/recession is defined as a prolonged increase (decline) in economic activity. The Economic Cycle Research Institute (ECRI) provides growth rate chronologies (http://www.businesscycle.com). According to ECRI, the rate of growth is computed as $[\frac{yt}{\sum_{j=0}^{s-1} y_{t-j}/s}]^{\frac{2s}{(s+1)}}$ where s is the number of observations. See Artis, Maecrellin, and Proietti (2003).

[6] This follows Pagan (2003).

2.1. The Deviation Cycle and the Classical Cycle

The Deviation Cycle, also known as the growth cycle, sees the cycle as a set of serially correlated deviations of a series from its trend (Lucas 1987; Sargent 1987; Blanchard and Fisher 1989; Kydland and Prescott 1990; Zarnowitz 1992). According to this approach, any series in levels (y_t) can be decomposed into a trend (μ_t) and cycle component (ψ_t). That is,

$$(1) y_t = \mu_t + \psi_t$$

Assuming that (y_t) is expressed in logarithm and that it admits the log-additive decomposition, growth (or the change in the logarithm of y_t, i.e., Δy_t) can then be decomposed in turn into a trend and a cycle component,

$$(2) \Delta y_t = \Delta \mu_t + \Delta \psi_t$$

Within this approach, an expansion occurs when growth of the series in question is above trend, i.e., $\Delta y_t > \Delta \mu_t$. Similarly, a recession occurs when the growth of a series is below trend, i.e., $\Delta y_t < \Delta \mu_t$. A central aspect of this approach is the construction of the permanent component of the series, which is usually derived using some type of filter.[7] On the basis of the above, deviation cycles are then constructed.

The Classical Cycle views the cycle as a set of turning points of a time series, representing the level of aggregate economic activity without consideration to a trend (Burns and Mitchell 1946;; Harding and Pagan 2002b, 2005; Pagan 2003). The inflection points of the series are then used as a basis to analyze the cycle in terms of a series of indicators such as the duration and intensity of an expansion (trough-to-peak) and a contraction (peak-to-trough), and the degree of coincidence between two given time series. Central to this approach is the identification of the turning points of a series.

The turning points of a series are usually identified using the Bry-Boschan algorithm (1971) developed originally for monthly data and adapted to deal with quarterly observation by Harding and Pagan (2002a).[8] The algorithm consists in identifying local maxima and minima for a given series following a logarithmic transformation using specific censoring rules (Bry-Boschan 1971; Du Plessis 2006; Male 2009).

---

[7] Including the band-pass (i.e., Baxter and King), Hodrick-Prescott, and model-based filters.
[8] The majority of recent Classical Cycle analyses use the Bry-Boschan algorithm for identifying turning points.

These include the specification of two quarters for a minimum duration for a single phase, and a minimum duration of five quarters for a complete cycle (Harding and Pagan 2002a). The peak for a series y_t is found when y_t is greater than $y_{t\mp k}$ for $k = 1,2$. Similarly, the trough for a series y_t is found when y_t is less than $y_{t\mp k}$ for $k = 1,2$. The algorithm excludes the occurrence of two successive peaks or troughs.

Two other alternative algorithms used in the literature on business cycles to determine turning points are the Calculus and the Okun rule. The Calculus rule identifies a recession (expansion) when the rate of growth of GDP is negative (positive) for at least one quarter. The Okun rule extends the time domain of an expansion or recession to two quarters (see Pagan 2003 ; see, also, Table 2).[9]

Table 2 Algorithms for the identification of turning points in Classical Cycles

Algorithms	Peak	Trough
Bry-Boschan	$\{(y_{t-2}, y_{t-1}) < y_t > (y_{t+1}, y_{t+2})\}$	$\{(y_{t-2}, y_{t-1}) > y_t < (y_{t+1}, y_{t+2})\}$
Calculus	$\{y_{t-1}, < y_t > y_{t+1},\}$	$\{y_{t-1}, > y_t < y_{t+1}\}$
Okun	$\{(\Delta y_{t-1}, \Delta y_t) > 0; (\Delta y_{t+1}, \Delta y_{t+2}) < 0\}$	$\{(\Delta y_{t-1}, \Delta y_t) < 0, (\Delta y_{t+1}, \Delta y_{t+2}) > 0\}$

Source: On the basis of Pagan 2003; Harding 2008; Wecker 1970.

Once the turning points in the series are identified, the business cycle can be characterized in terms of duration and intensity. The duration (D) of an expansion is defined as the ratio the total number of quarters of expansion to the total number of peaks. That is,

$$(3) D = \frac{\sum_{t=1}^{T} S_t}{\sum_{t=1}^{T-1}(1 - S_{t+1})S_t}$$

---

[9] As can be seen from the definition, the Calculus criterion tends to produce a higher frequency of expansions and contractions than the Bry-Boschan or the Okun criteria, simply because its threshold to identify whether a series is in a contraction or an expansion phase is comparatively less demanding. It requires only one observation where the growth of the series in question is negative ($\Delta y_t < 0$), whereas the Bry-Boschan and Okun require two consecutive observations.

where S is a binary variable that takes a 1 during an expansion and 0 during a contraction.[10] The numerator in (1) ($\sum_{t=1}^{T} S_t$) denotes the total duration of expansions and the denominator ($\sum_{t=1}^{T-1}(1 - S_{t+1})S_t$) measures the number of peaks in the series.

For its part, the intensity or amplitude (A) of the expansion is measured as the ratio of the total change in aggregate economic activity to the total number of peaks. That is,

$$(4)\ A = \frac{\sum_{t=1}^{T} S_t \Delta Y_t}{\sum_{t=1}^{T-1}(1 - S_{t+1})S_t}$$

where Y is a measure of economic activity (GDP in our cases) and the numerator in (4) ($\sum_{t=1}^{T} S_t \Delta Y_t$) is the total change in economic activity.

Using Harding and Pagan's triangle analogy, the ratio of the amplitude to the duration can be thought of as a measure of steepness. Also, the cumulative change (CC) in the expansion (contraction) can then be found by multiplying the product of the duration (D) and the intensity (A) of the expansion (contraction) by 0.5, i.e, CC = 0.5*(D*A).

Due to the differences in their definition of the cycle, the application of a similar methodology (say, that of the Bry-Boschan algorithm, as is done throughout this paper) to identify the turning points in the Classical and Deviation Cycle analyses can produce different characterizations of the cycle. Two of these differences are worth noting.

First, the Classical Cycle tends to produce shorter contractions than the Deviation Cycle. This is due to the fact that a downturn in the Classical Cycle occurs when $\Delta y_t < 0$. Contrarily, in the Deviation Cycle, a downturn occurs when $\Delta y_t - \Delta \mu_t < 0$. This implies that a downward phase in a Deviation Cycle can contain several Classical Cycle recession episodes (see Artis, Maecrellin and Proietti, 2003al. 2011 and Pagan 2003). [11]

Second, the Deviation Cycle fails to capture the asymmetry between the contraction and the expansion phases. This responds to the fact that the Deviation Cycle is defined as a series of correlated deviations from the trend. As a result, the cyclical component is stationary, and this implies that the long-run average of the cyclical

---

[10] Similarly, the duration and amplitude for contractions are computed using $c_{i,t} = 1 - s_{i.t}$.

[11] A deviation cycle considers as a recession not only the case in which $\Delta y_t < 0$, as in the Classical Cycle, but also when $\Delta y_t > 0$ and $|\Delta \mu_t| > |\Delta y_t|$. In this sense, these methods are not strictly comparable. Pagan (2003, p. 17) states that: "…those statistics gathered about the business cycle by Burns and Mitchell and the NBER have no immediate relevance to those of the [the Deviation Cycle]." In this paper, the aim of using different methodologies is mainly to show that the results obtained are robust to different methodologies. Even though we make comparisons in the text among methodologies, the guiding principle is to assess them for their own logic and development.

component is zero.[12] That is, the positive and negative deviations will tend to cancel out over time. Thus by virtue of its own definition, the positive and negative cyclical deviations from the trend are symmetric.

Cognizant of these differences, we assess the results of each of these criteria and approaches on the basis of their own terms and logic. It is a question of identifying stylized facts pertaining to the specific behavior of the Latin America and Caribbean cycles in comparison to other regions that are robust with regard to the use of different statistical methodologies.

2.2. The dataset

In order to ensure adequate geographical representation, a comprehensive sample of 83 countries was used in the analysis. Of these, 44 are emerging market economies and 39 are considered developed economies (i.e., high-income economies).[13] The analysis is undertaken using quarterly data for the period 1989–2012.[14]

The sample of emerging market economies comprise 21 countries belonging to Latin America and the Caribbean, 5 to East Asia and the Pacific, 11 to Europe and Central Asia, 3 to the Middle East and North Africa, 1 to South Asia, and 3 to Sub-Saharan Africa. The sub-sample of high-income economies includes European (23), Asian (4), North American (2), Caribbean (2), and other countries.[15]

---

[12] In the Deviation Cycle, the cyclical component is stationary. Stationarity is not an issue in the Classical Cycle approach.

[13] As noted above, our analysis includes only low- and upper- and low-middle-income countries in the category of emerging market economies. This marks a difference between our approach and other studies that tend to include countries such as Singapore and Hong Kong as emerging market economies, and thus end up comparing the performance of middle-income countries, such as those of Latin America, with both middle-income and high-income countries indistinctively.

[14] Data for the period 1989–2012 was not available for all countries. See the appendix for a detailed overview of the countries included and the respective time period. Quarterly GDP was used for all countries in the sample, with the only exception of Barbados. In the case of Barbados, due to data limitations, quarterly GDP was proxied by tourist arrivals. In Barbados, the data available on a yearly basis for tourist arrivals and GDP show that both variables exhibit a high degree of coincidence (including turning points) and association (very high and significant correlation coefficient).

[15] The other countries include Cyprus, Israel, Macao, and Malta. The Caribbean countries include: Barbados, Belize, the Dominican Republic, Grenada, Jamaica, St. Lucia, Trinidad, and Tobago.

Table 3 Data sample for selected studies on business cycles

	Countries	EME	EME Regions						DC	Period/ periodicity	Variables
			EAP	ECA	MENA	SSA	SA	LAC			
Current paper	83	**44**	5	11	3	3	1	21	39	**1989.1– 2012.2 Quarterly**	**GDP**
Titelman, Pérez Caldentey, Carvallo (2011)	63	37	4	8	2	1	1	20	31	1990–2010 Quarterly	GDP, C, I, X, M, G
Male (2009))	35	27	2	4	4	5	3	9	8	1960.1– 2005.4 Quarterly	Industrial & agricultural output
Du Plessis (2006)	24	2	1	...	...	1	...	2	22	1970.1– 2005.1 Quarterly	GDP, C, I, π, r, FS
Cashin (2004)	10	6	...	...	...	...	...	6	4	1963–2003 Yearly	GDP
Craigwell & Maurin (2012)	3	3	...	...	...	...	...	3	...	Quarterly	GDP
Calderón & Fuentes (2012)	65	32	5	9	3	2	...	13	34	1970.1– 2010.2 Quarterly	GDP
Calderón & Fuentes (2010)	45	19	4	1	...	1	1	12	16	1980.1– 2006.2 Quarterly	GDP
Rand & Tarp (2002)	15	14	1	...	1	5	2	5	1	1960.1– 1999.4 Quarterly	Industrial production Index
Pérez Caldentey & Pineda (2011)	134	104	19	20	13	15	5	32	31	1950–2011 Yearly	GDP, GDP per capita

Note: EME = emerging market economies; EAP = East Asia and Pacific; ECA = Europe and Central Asia; MENA = Middle East and North Africa; SSA = Sub-Saharan Africa; SA = South Asia; LAC= Latin America and the Caribbean; DC = Developed countries. In our approach, developed countries are high income countries; GDP = Gross Domestic Product; C = private consumption; G = government consumption; I = gross formation of fixed capital; X = exports; M = imports; π = inflation, r = nominal rate of interest, FS = measure of the fiscal stance. The periodicity refers to the most ample data range used in each specific paper. *Source:* Authors' own computations

As can be seen from Table 3, our dataset is (in comparison to other analyses on the subject) one of the largest and most representative at the regional and also at the Latin American and Caribbean sub-regional level. In contrast to other studies on the subject, it includes most countries of South and Central America as well as Caribbean economies, thus avoiding introducing a sub-regional bias in the results obtained.[16]

3. The stylized facts of the expansionary and contractionary phases of the Latin American and Caribbean cycle

In comparison to other developed and developing regions of the world, the business cycle of expansions and contractions of Latin America and the Caribbean displays two distinctive features. First, as a general rule, the region has weaker expansions than other developing regions—East Asia and the Pacific, in particular. Second, Latin America and the Caribbean have, on average, contractions in terms of duration and amplitude that tend to converge to those of other countries, both developed and developing. These results are robust in terms of the business cycle methodology used.[17] Both of these stylized facts are analyzed in detail in the sections that follow.

3.1. The expansionary phase of the cycle

The comparative analysis of expansions using the two-cycle methodologies shows that Latin America and the Caribbean have shorter and less intense expansions relative to other regions of the world.

In terms of duration, the Classical Methodology (using the Bry-Boschan algorithm) shows that Latin America and the Caribbean expansionary periods span, on average, a period of 14 quarters (3.5 years).[18] With the exception of the Middle East and North Africa (one year), Latin America and the Caribbean's expansion performance is shorter than that of the rest of the regions considered, and in particular than that of East Asia and the Pacific. In the case of East Asia and the Pacific, expansions last nearly eight

---

[16] Calderón and Fuentes (2010, 2012) include only one country from Central America, Costa Rica, which may help to explain that their results seem to be representative mostly of the South American Cycle.

[17] The results by region refer to medians in order to deal with outliers because the distribution of the observation in terms of amplitude and duration (except perhaps for the duration of the contraction) are skewed.

[18] The Bry-Boschan algorithm to identify turning points was used for both Classical and Deviation Cycle methodologies. These were obtained using MatLab with the help of computer codes provided by Professors John Rand and Finn Tarp (Univesity of Conpenhagen). Stata was used for the identification of turning points using the Okun and Calculus algorithms and to compute the cycle indicators.

years, which is almost five years longer than in the case of Latin America and the Caribbean. For the high-income countries, the duration of the expansion is also longer (6 years or roughly two more years than in the case of Latin America and the Caribbean). The Deviation Cycle methodology corroborates the result that, with the exception of the Middle East and North Africa, Latin America and the Caribbean has one of the shortest expansions among the developing world (Table 4).

Table 4 Duration and amplitude of the expansionary phase of the cycle for selected regions of the world, 1990–2012 (quarterly data)

Duration (in quarters)				
	Classical Cycle			Deviation Cycle
	Bry-Boschan	Calculus	Okun	Bry-Boschan
East Asia and the Pacific	32.5	7.7	27.0	9.3
Europe and Central Asia	25.0	4.4	22.5	8.7
Latin America and the Caribbean	13.6	4.4	10.8	7.5
Middle East and North Africa	3.5	5.4	35.5	5.8
South Asia	...	48.0	...	8.5
Sub-Saharan Africa	37.5	2.4	11.0	8.0
High Income	23.0	5.0	13.3	7.7
Amplitude (In percentages)				
	Classical Cycle			Deviation Cycle
	Bry-Boschan	Calculus	Okun	Bry-Boschan
East Asia and the Pacific	39.0	11.1	29.2	5.8
Europe and Central Asia	43.8	10.1	39.4	9.1
Latin America and the Caribbean	26.3	8.1	16.2	5.8
Middle East and North Africa	15.6	9.5	33.0	4.0
South Asia	...	85.6	...	3.2
Sub-Saharan Africa	40.9	9.0	12.9	3.9
High Income	26.3	6.4	14.1	4.5

Source: Authors' own computations
Note: '...' denotes not available.

The cycle analysis of the most recent expansion does not alter our conclusions. For the majority of Latin American and the Caribbean, the most recent expansion began in the early 2000s and ended with the Global Financial Crisis (2009). It was one of the longest and most intense expansions in over three decades. However, this expansion episode falls short both in terms of duration and amplitude when compared to the last expansion episode of other regions, and in particular to that of East Asia and the Pacific (26.5 quarters and 29.8 percent for Latin America and the Caribbean and 40 quarters and 53.9 percent for East Asia and the Pacific respectively).[19]

In line with the above results, Latin America and Caribbean also exhibits one of the weakest output gains in the expansionary phase of the cycle. This result holds mostly for the Classical Cycle methodologyin its different turning point algorithms.

The Classical Cycle (using the Bry-Boschan algorithm) shows that, on average, Latin America and the Caribbean register a 26.3 percent increase in output, respectively. This contrasts with the experience of our benchmark region, East Asia and the Pacific, which records a 39 percent output gain (50 percent above that of Latin America and the Caribbean). In the case of the Deviation Cycle, Latin America and the Caribbean's amplitude during the expansionary phase is similar to that of East Asia and the Pacific and is below that of Europe and Central Asia.

In any case, the weaker performance of Latin American and Caribbean economies relative to other regions in the expansionary phase of the cycle is underscored when viewed in terms of the cumulative gain in outputFigure 1 shows the gain in cumulative output of East Asia and the Pacific and high-income countries relative to that of Latin America using an average of all criteria used in the paper[20]. East Asia and the Pacific have a gain in output that is, almost thrice that of Latin America and the Caribbean. For its part, the gain in output of the high-income economies grouping is 10 percent higher relative to that of Latin America and the Caribbean (Figure 1).

---

[19] These numbers refer to the duration and amplitude of a single episode. They refer to the numerator of the duration and amplitude formulas (Equations 3 and 4 above), and in this sense are not strictly comparable to the rest of the cycle indicators provided in the paper. In the case of Europe and Central Asia, the duration and amplitude of the last expansion episode are also greater than those of Latin America and the Caribbean (36.5 quarters and 63.2 percent).

[20] Using only the Deviation Cycle methodology the cumulative again in output is also larger for East Asia and the Pacific in relation to Latin America and the Caribbean.

Figure 1 Average cumulative output gain of East Asia and the Pacific and the high-income country grouping relative to Latin America and the Caribbean (1990–2012)

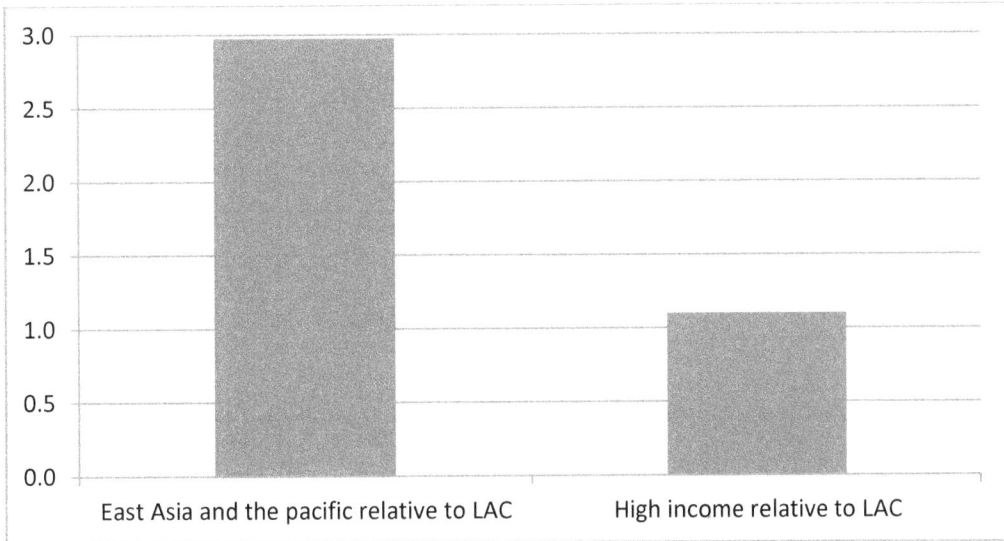

Note: Refers to the average of the Bry-Boschan, Calculus, Okun and Cycle Deviation for the period 1990–2012.The cumulative output gain is computed as the product of the amplitude and duration of the expansion phase of East Asia and high-income economies relative to that of Latin America and the Caribbean.

Source: Authors' own computations

The application of our approach separately to South America, Central America, and Mexico does not change the results found at the regional level. The duration of the expansion for South America, Central America, and Mexico is 15, 25, and 23, quarters respectively. The amplitude of their expansion reaches 28 percent, 27 percent, and 26 percent, respectively (Table 5).

Table 5 Duration and amplitude of the expansionary phase of the cycle for Latin America and the Caribbean and its sub-regions 1990–2012

Duration (In quarters)				
	Classical Cycle			Deviation Cycle
	Bry-Boschan	Calculus	Okun	Bry-Boschan
Latin America and the Caribbean	13.6	4.4	10.8	7.5
South America	15.3	4.8	13.1	7.8
Central America	25.0	4.5	27.0	7.5
Mexico	23.0	5.1	11.0	11.3
Amplitude (In percentages)				
	Classical Cycle			Deviation Cycle
	Bry-Boschan	Calculus	Okun	Bry-Boschan
Latin America and the Caribbean	26.3	8.1	16.2	5.8
South America	27.9	7.8	14.7	5.8
Central America	27.0	8.4	29.2	4.9
Mexico	25.6	6.9	15.3	6.2

Source: Authors' own.computations.

Further corroborating evidence regarding the limited nature of the expansion in Latin America is provided by the disaggregation of this phase of the cycle into its two sub-phases, acceleration and deceleration. Acceleration is defined by a GDP growing at an increasing rate, or, in other words, by a first and second positive derivative of the GDP level series. Deceleration refers to a GDP growing at decreasing rates, or, in other words, the first derivative of the GDP series in levels is positive, while the second derivative is negative.

As shown in Figure 2, Latin America and the Caribbean have one the weakest rates of growth for both the acceleration and deceleration sub-phases in comparison to other developing and developed regions. The average rate of growth in the acceleration phase reaches 6.1 percent for Latin America and the Caribbean, while for other regions such as East Asia and the Pacific, it reaches roughly 7 percent. In a similar way, Latin

America also experiences a slower deceleration phase than other regions, with the exception of Middle East and North Africa and Sub-Saharan Africa.

Figure 2 Average rate of growth of GDP during the acceleration and deceleration sub-phases of the cycle for selected developing regions of the world, 1990–2012

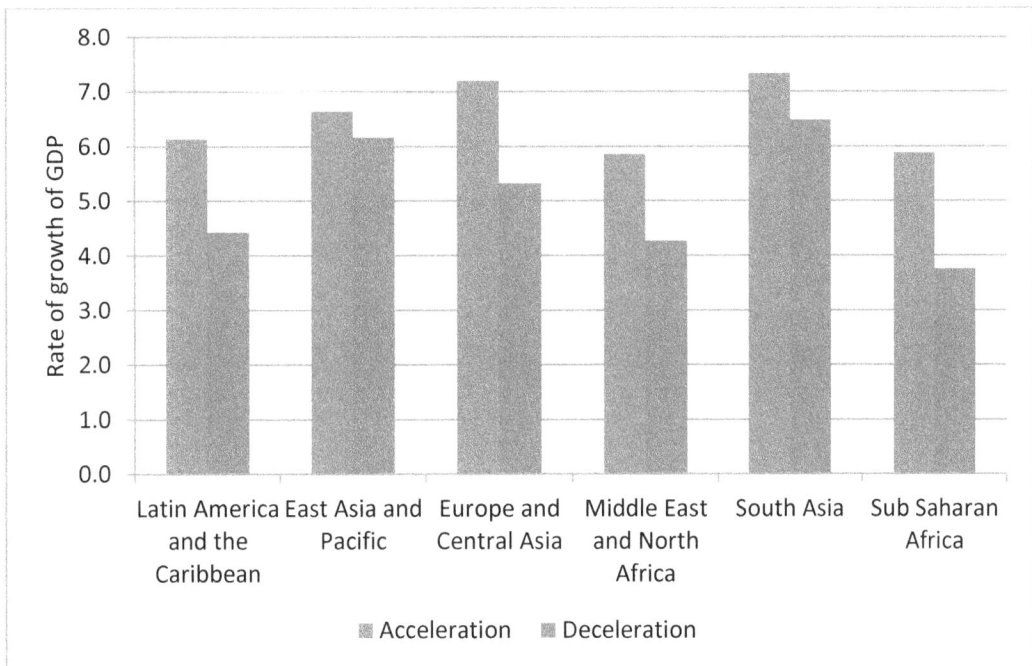

Source: Authors' own computations

3.2. The contraction phase of the economic cycle

In contrast to the results obtained for the expansions, the duration and intensity of the contraction for Latin American and Caribbean countries tends to conform to those found for other regions according to both the Classical and Deviation Cycle methodologies.

In the case of the Classical Cycle methodology, the Bry-Boschan algorithm estimates that, with the exception of the Middle East and North Africa, the duration of contractions is less than a year. These range between 2.7 to 3.8 quarters (that is, between 8 and 11 months). The duration of contractions for Latin America and the Caribbean, Europe and Central Asia, and East Asia and the Pacific are very similar, between 3.3 and 3.8 quarters, or between 10 to 11 months.

The Okun and Calculus criterion yield a higher degree of uniformity in the duration of contractions among developing regions, and according to both, the experience of Latin America and the Caribbean also conforms to the results found for other developing regions (Table 6).

Table 6 Duration and amplitude of the contractionary phase of the cycle for selected regions of the world, 1990–2012 (quarterly data)

	Duration (In quarters)			
	Classical Cycle			Deviation Cycle
	Bry-Boschan	Calculus	Okun	Bry-Boschan
East Asia and the Pacific	3.3	1.6	2.2	4.8
Europe and Central Asia	3.8	1.6	3.3	5.3
Latin America and the Caribbean	3.8	1.6	3.3	6.0
Middle East and North Africa	7.3	1.2	2.8	6.5
South Asia	…	1.0	…	6.7
Sub-Saharan Africa	2.7	1.3	2.5	5.3
High Income	4.0	1.6	3.4	6.3
	Amplitude (In percentages)			
	Classical Cycle			Deviation Cycle
	Bry-Boschan	Calculus	Okun	Bry-Boschan
East Asia and the Pacific	-10.6	-3.7	-4.4	-5.8
Europe and Central Asia	-11.6	-4.6	-7.1	-9.6
Latin America and the Caribbean	-4.6	-2.1	-3.2	-6.2
Middle East and North Africa	-7.0	-1.2	0.3	-3.8
South Asia	…	-0.2	…	-2.9
Sub-Saharan Africa	-7.1	-1.7	-1.4	-3.8
High Income	-4.9	-1.8	-2.6	-4.3

Note: … denotes not available.

Source: Authors' own computations

The application of the Deviation Cycle methodology corroborates the above findings. Contractions tend to last for a similar length of time and the Latin America and the Caribbean region is not an exception to this rule.[21]

Figure 3 Asymmetry of the duration of the cycle based on the Deviation from Trend and Classical Cycle Analysis, selected regions of the world (1990–2012, averages based on quarterly data) *Source:* Authors' own computations

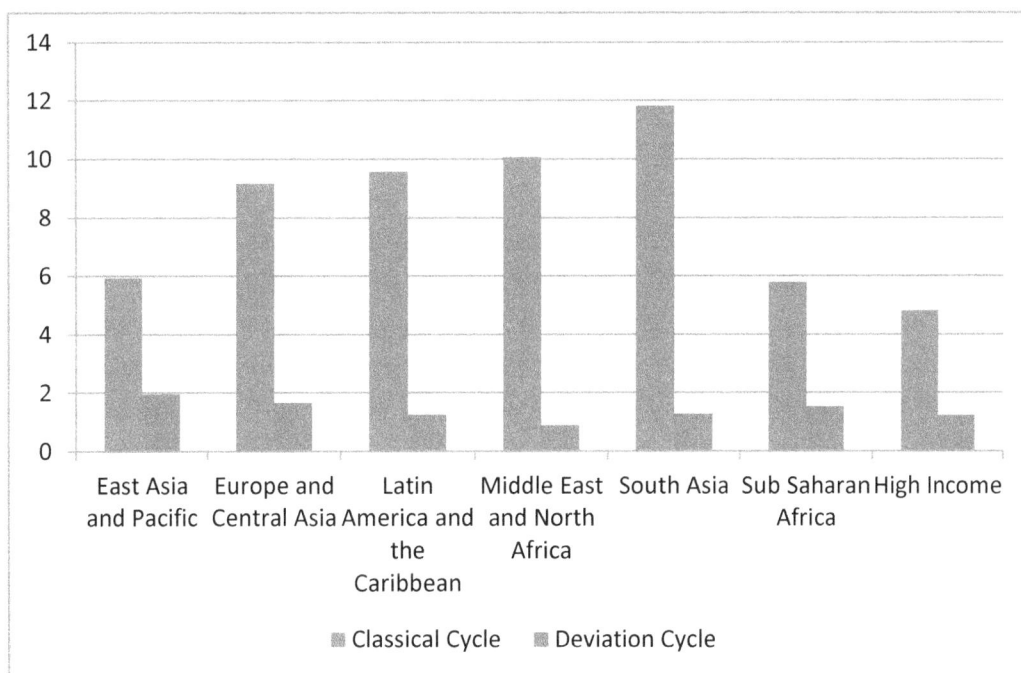

Moreover, as explained earlier, due to the fact that the Deviation Cycle approach sees the cycle as a stationary process, whereby the deviations from trend cancel each other out over time, it does not capture the asymmetry of the cycle. Indeed, as shown in Figure 3 above, the duration of the expansion relative to that of the contraction is very similar for all regions, nearing a value of one (i.e., the expansions last as long as the contractions). This contrasts with the Classical Cycle methodology where the contraction and the

---

[21] However, this methodology, as explained in Section 1.1, tends to produce longer contractions across all regions than the Classical Cycle methodology (see Pagan 2003 on this point). Indeed, contractions according to this methodology tend to last for at least five quarters in most cases.

expansion are independent events. The standard deviation for the duration of the contraction using the Classical Cycle methodology equals 2.64, while for the Deviation from Trend, it is equal to 0.34 (see Figure 3).

In line with these results, contractions do not prove to be more intense in the case of Latin America and the Caribbean in relation to other regions. As shown in Table 6 above, according to the Bry-Boschan algorithm used in the Classical Cycle approach, Latin America and the Caribbean have the smallest amplitude of contractions among all developing and developed regions. The average amplitude of the contractions equals 4.6 percent for Latin America and the Caribbean. This nears that of the high-income country grouping (4.9 percent) and falls below that of East Asian and Pacific (10.6 percent), Europe and Central Asia (11.6 percent), Middle East and North Africa (7.0 percent), and Sub-Saharan Africa (7.1 percent).

According to the two other criteria (Calculus and Okun), the amplitude of the contraction in Latin America and the Caribbean is below that of East Asia and the Pacific, and Europe and Central Asia.

The findings of the Deviation Cycle approach are not as clear cut. The intensity of the contraction for Latin America and the Caribbean is below that of Europe and Central Asia, similar to that of East Asia and the Pacific, and surpasses that of the rest of the regions.

A more detailed analysis for Latin America by sub-regions (South America, Central America, Caribbean), indicates that the dispersion of the amplitude in the case of a contraction is higher than that of an expansion. South America and Mexico seem to have more pronounced and sharp contractions relative to Central America and the Caribbean. In the cases of South America and Mexico, the amplitude is equal to 7.1 percent and 7.9 percent using the Bry-Boschan criterion, and 2.4 percent and 2.6 percent using the Calculus criterion. For their part, the respective amplitudes for Central America and the Caribbean using both criteria are 3.8 percent, 5.4 percent, and 1.3 percent and 3.1 percent, respectively (Table 7).[22]

---

[22] The Caribbean includes the Dominican Republic.

Table 7 Amplitude of the contractionary phase of the cycle for Latin America and the Caribbean and its sub-regions, 1990–2012 (in percentages using quarterly data)

	Bry-Boschan	Calculus
Latin America and the Caribbean	-4.6	-2.1
South America	-7.1	-2.4
Central America	-3.8	-1.2
México	-7.9	-2.6
Caribbean	-5.4	-3.1

Source: Authors' own.computations

This difference at the sub-regional level is explained by the fact that the strongest and most intense crises in the period under study—the Mexican crisis (1994–1995), the Asian crisis (1997–1998), the Russian crisis (1998) and the Argentine crisis (2001–2002)—had their epicenter in Mexico or South America.

4. The complete Latin American and Caribbean cycle of expansions and contractions

Both of the stylized facts analyses above (weaker expansions and convergent contractions) imply that the complete Latin America and the Caribbean cycle exhibits, for the most part, the shortest duration and smallest amplitude in relation to other regions.

The length of the duration of an entire cycle using the Classical Cycle methodology (and, as a reference, the Bry-Boschan criterion) is roughly 17 quarters for Latin America and the Caribbean. This is below that found for high-income countries (27 quarters) and also for the majority of developing regions. In the particular case of East Asia and the Pacific, our benchmark, the cycle lasts 36 quarters, that is, almost five years longer than that of Latin America and the Caribbean (Table 8).

These results do not change in any significant manner when the comparison is undertaken using the Deviation Cycle analysis. This shows that with the exception of the Middle East and North Africa, Latin America and the Caribbean has the shortest cycle of all the regions included in the exercise.[23]

---

[23] Throughout the paper, the Deviation Cycles are computed using the Hodrick-Prescott filter. Some authors suggest that the difference in duration, especially between developed and developing economies, is due to a lack of homogeneity in the data, and in particular of using industrial activity

Table 8 Duration (in quarters) of the complete cycle on a regional basis, 1990-2012 (quarterly data)

Region	Classical Cycle			Deviation Cycle
	Bry-Boschan	**Calculus**	**Okun**	**Bry-Boschan**
East Asia and the Pacific	35.8	9.3	29.2	14.0
Europe and Central Asia	28.8	6.1	25.8	13.9
Latin America and the Caribbean	**17.4**	**6.0**	**14.1**	**13.5**
Middle East and North Africa	10.8	6.5	38.3	12.3
South Asia	...	49.0	...	15.2
Sub-Saharan Africa	40.2	3.7	13.5	13.3
High Income	27.0	6.6	16.7	14.0

Note: ... denotes not available.

Source: Authors' own computations

At the same time that Latin America exhibits the shortest duration of cycles, it also displays, using the smallest amplitude, that is the shortest distance between the intensity of the contraction and that of the expansion according the Classical Cycle methodology. Taking East Asia and the Pacific as a reference point, the amplitude of its cycle is 60 percent greater than that of Latin American and the Caribbean. (Table 9).

---

indices for developing countries and GDP data for developed countries. See Male (2009) and Du Plessis (2006). Our results are not affected by the use of GDP or of an index of industrial production. Using the latter measure, Latin America and the Caribbean still exhibits the shortest full cycle duration.

Table 9 Amplitude of the complete cycle on a regional basis, 1990–2012 (in percentage using quarterly data)

Region	Classical Cycle			Deviation Cycle
	Bry-Boschan	Calculus	Okun	Bry-Boschan
East Asia and the Pacific	49.6	14.8	33.5	11.6
Europe and Central Asia	55.4	14.7	46.6	18.7
Latin America and the Caribbean	**30.9**	**10.3**	**19.3**	**12.0**
Middle East and North Africa	22.5	10.6	32.7	7.7
South Asia	...	85.8	...	6.1
Sub-Saharan Africa	48.0	10.6	14.3	7.7
High Income	31.1	8.2	16.7	8.8

Note: ... denotes not available.

Source: Authors' own.computations

5. Cycles and long-run outcomes: conceptual issues and some preliminary evidence

The specific characteristics of the cycle for Latin America and Caribbean countries and, in particular, the weak nature of expansions are not confined to short-run analysis. They are also reflected in the behavior of variables such as productivity and investment, which have an impact on long-run growth trajectories. In this sense, we follow the more recent literature that establishes a connection between cyclical fluctuations and long-term outcomes (Dickens and Madrick 2010; Dutt and Ros 2009; Aghion, Hemous, and Kharroubi 2010, IMF 2009; European Commission 2009). [24]

Table 10 shows the duration and amplitude of the expansion for labor productivity for Latin America and the Caribbean countries in comparison to the rest of the countries included in our sample. Independently of the cycle methodology used, and in line with our

---

[24] Part of this literature sustains that shocks such as wars, natural disasters, financial crisis, and, in general contractions, in economic activity can lead to income per capita divergence by causing permanent losses in trend output and lower long-run growth. The specificities and transmission mechanisms include, among others, the effect of aggregate demand fluctuactions on the capital stock, investment, and labor (e.g, Dutt and Ros 2009, IMF 2009), financing constraints (Aghion, Hemous, and Kharroubi 2010), or the impact on total factor producticity or the permanent destruction of human capital (European Comission 2009). Another transmission mechanism is volatility (Ramey and Ramey 1995; Turnovsky & Chattopadhyay, P, (1998) 1998, Yigit 2003).

previous results, Latin America and the Caribbean have, for the most part, one of the shortest expansions in productivity growth.

Table 10 Duration and amplitude of the expansionary phase of the labor productivity cycle for selected regions of the world using the Classical Cycle methodology, 1990–2012 (yearly data)

	Duration (In years)	
	Bry-Boschan	Calculus
East Asia and the Pacific	4.3	4.3
Europe and Central Asia	5.5	5.5
Latin America and the Caribbean	3.8	3.8
Middle East and North Africa	3.3	3.3
South Asia	4.8	4.7
Sub-Saharan Africa	2.6	2.6
High Income	6.3	6.3
	Amplitude (In percentages)	
	Bry-Boschan	Calculus
East Asia and the Pacific	23.4	23.4
Europe and Central Asia	33.7	33.7
Latin America and the Caribbean	13.6	13.6
Middle East and North Africa	17.2	17.2
South Asia	16.0	15.2
Sub-Saharan Africa	8.5	8.5
High Income	17.7	17.6

Note: Labor productivity refers to labor productivity per person employed in 2011 US$ (converted to 2011 price level with updated 2005 EKS PPPs).
Source: Authors' own.computations

In this regard, the differences between the cumulative gain (the product of the amplitude and the duration) in productivity between Latin America and the Caribbean and East Asia and the Pacific are worth highlighting. The cumulative gain in labor productivity during the expansionary phase of the cycle is 25 percent for Latin America and the Caribbean and twice this figure (50 percent) in the case of East Asia and the Pacific.

Jointly with the fact that Latin America and the Caribbean experience weaker expansions than other regions and, in particular, than East Asia and the Pacific, this type of evidence may help to explain the reason why the countries of East Asia and the Pacific have been able to sustain over time a high GDP growth path relative to the case of Latin America and the Caribbean. This is shown in Figure 4, which plots the trend of GDP for the period 1960–2010 for both regions.

Figure 4 GDP trend for Latin America and the Caribbean and East Asia and the Pacific, 1960–2010 (logarithmic scale, annual data)

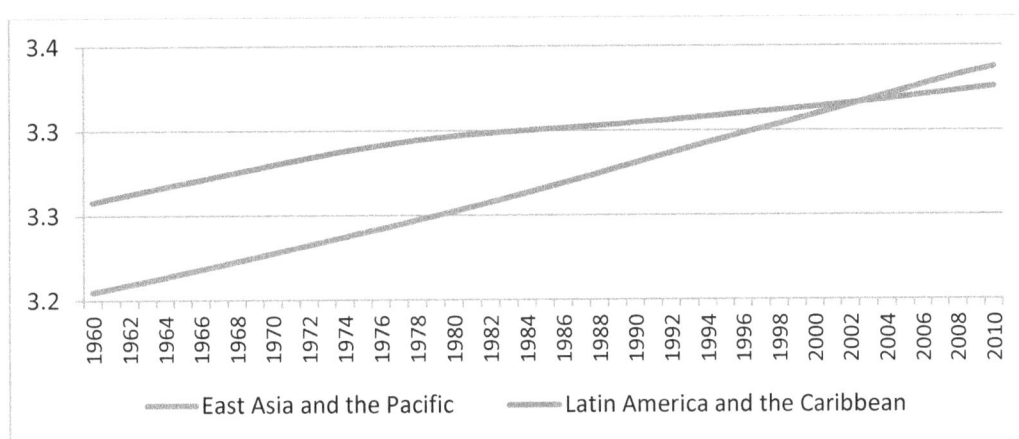

Note: The computations were undertaken using the Deviation Cycle methodology.
Source: Economic Commission for Latin America and the Caribbean (ECLAC), on the basis of World Bank, "World Development Indicators" and "Global Finance" [online] http://www.gfmag.com/.

Whereas the East Asia and Pacific region has been able to maintain a rising trajectory throughout the period, Latin America and the Caribbean experience a structural break in the 1980s, due most likely to the effects of the debt crisis, from which the region has not been able to recover in the following two decades. At a more detailed level of analysis, the figure shows that the GDP trend between 1960 and the early 1980s (period I) of Latin America and the Caribbean is similar to that in East Asia and the Pacific. Then, starting with the lost decade of the 1980s, it tends to decline and does not recover in the 1990s or the first decade of the 2000s, meaning that in this sub-period growth rates are lower than before the debt crisis (period II).

The long-term effects of the crisis are seen in the structural break in the region's GDP trend. At the same time, the weak nature of recoveries is underscored by the fact that the economic policies implemented in the two decades after the crisis did not reverse those effects. Even in the period of fastest growth witnessed by Latin America and the Caribbean over the past 30 years (2003–2008), the countries of the region, with few exceptions, did not succeed in reversing the structural break or improving the trend. This is unlike what happened in Asia: the 1997 crisis, one of the severest to hit the countries of East Asia, did not change the path of trend GDP.

An additional piece of evidence linking the fluctuations of the cycle to long-run growth is provided by the behavior of public investment, which is also clearly asymmetric, with drops during recessions being much sharper than increases during upswings. As shown in Table 11 considering data for six countries in the region, public investment in infrastructure fell by an average of 36 percent in the downswing of the business cycle.[25]

Table 11 Latin America (selected countries): duration and amplitude of expansions and contractions of the cycle of public investment in infrastructure, 1980–2010 (yearly data)

	Expansion		Contraction	
	Duration	Amplitude	Duration	Amplitude
Total	2.7	25.6	2.2	-35.6
Energy sector	1.9	34.7	2.0	-51.5
Roads and railways	2.1	32.3	1.7	-33.1
Telecommunications	1.8	28.1	1.9	-58.0
Water and sanitation	1.6	24.2	1.7	-23.8

Note: The Bry-Boschan algorithm was used for identifying the turning points.
Source: Economic Commission for Latin America and the Caribbean (ECLAC) 2012.,

Declines in public infrastructure investment tend to be sharper than any increase during the recovery phase. In the sectors considered, the contraction is, on average, 40 percent greater than the subsequent expansion. In the power and telecommunications sectors, the difference between the decline in investment during a contraction and the increase

---

[25] Argentina, Brazil, Chile, Colombia, Mexico, and Peru, which account for 85.5 percent of the region's GDP between them.

during the expansion is even greater (35 percent increase and -52 percent decline for the energy sector and 28 percent and -58 percent for the telecommunications sector, respectively). Such a pattern has negative impacts on capital accumulation over time.

The contraction in investment can have short-run effects on aggregate demand, but it also has an impact on the long-run trajectory of the economy. This is due not only to the fact that public investment contributes to the growth of the economy, but also to the fact that investment in decisions, in general, are often irreversible ("once installed, capital has little or no value unless used in production") and this characteristic provides a link between the decisions taken in the short run with medium- and long-run outcomes.

Irreversibility can often become an important factor in the decision not to invest in the downward phase of the cycle due, for example, to the growing risks associated with the current and future macroeconomic context. In this sense, a downward phase of the business cycle can be associated with a low capital accumulation, which, in turn, results in furthering the decline in investment, undermining not only the job creating capacity of the economy, but also its recovery potential.

6. Conclusion: where we are and thoughts for further research

This paper shows that independently of the methodology adopted, the Latin American and Caribbean cycle exhibits two distinctive features. The first and most important one is that Latin America and the Caribbean register weaker expansions than those of other regions and, in particular, than those of the East Asian and Pacific region. The most recent expansion (2003–2007), which is by far one of the most intense in the history of the region, does not alter this conclusion in the sense that during period, Latin America and the Caribbean's rate of growth remained below that of other developing regions. A second distinctive feature is that Latin America and the Caribbean's contractions conform in terms of duration and amplitude to those of the rest of the world.

Weaker expansions and convergent contractions imply, as a result, that the complete cycle of expansions and contractions tends to be shorter and with a smaller amplitude for Latin America and the Caribbean relative to other regions of the world.

Traditionally, cycle patterns are viewed as short-run demand-led phenomena with no bearing on growth trends. However, this paper argues that the specificities of the cycle are not only relevant to the short-run. They are also reflected in the behavior of variables such as productivity and investment, which are linked to long-run growth performance.

In the particular case of Latin America and the Caribbean, the behavior of both productivity and investment reflect the weak nature of the region's expansions. In fact, the study of the particularities of the cycle, including weak expansions in output and productivity, may be central to explain, at least in part, the reason why the region has not been able to sustain growth concomitantly to other regions and, in particular, to East Asia and the Pacific.

The findings presented in this paper open important avenues to explore further and analyze the short- and long-term performance of Latin America and Caribbean economies.

First, cycle analysis should increase its focus on the nature and behavior of expansions. Sustaining evidence is provided by the fact that contractions tend to be somewhat homogeneous across regions in terms of duration and amplitude. However, this is not the case with expansions. Expansions are heterogeneous in terms of duration and amplitude. Improving our understanding of the differences in the expansionary dynamics of countries and regions can further our understanding of the differences in their rates of growth and levels of development, including those of Latin America and the Caribbean.

Second, as it is well established, the management of the cycle affects the short-run fluctuations of economic activity and, hence, volatility. But additionally, it is not trend-neutral. Hence, the effects of aggregate demand management policies may be more persistent over time and less transitory than currently thought to be. This provides a justification to reconsider the usefulness of stabilization policies and their effects, from a short- and long-run view, including their potential trade-offs, and to re-think how to articulate and coordinate what are currently called demand-side with supply-side policies.

References

Aghion, Philippe, Hemous, David, Kharroubi, Enisee (2010) Cyclical Fiscal Policy, Creditm Constraints, and Industry Growth. *BIS Working Paper No. 340*

Artis, M.; Maecrellin, M., & Proietti, T. (2003) Dating the Europ Area Business Cycle. http://www.eui.eu/Personal/Marcellino/23.pdf

Blanchard, O & Fischer, S. (1989) Lectures of Macroeconomics. Cambridge: MIT Press.

Bry, G & Boschan, C. (1971) Cyclical analysis of time series:selected procedures and computer programmes. New York, National Buraeu of Economic Research.

Burns, Arthur, E. and Mitchell, Wesley, C. (1946) Measuring Business Cycles. New York: NBER.

Calderón, C. & Fuentes, J.R. (2010) Characterizing the Business Cycles of Emerging Economies. Pontificia Universidad Católica de Chile. Instituto de Economía. Documento de Trabajo No. 371.

http://www.webmeets.com/files/papers/LACEALAMES/2012/495/Calderon%20Fuentes%20Cycles%20%2819%20March%202012%29.pdf

Calderón, C. & Fuentes, J.R. (2012) Have business cycles changed over the last two decades? AN Emprirical Investigation.

Cashin, P. (2004) Caribbean Business Cycles. IMF Working Paper. WP/04/136.

Craigwell, R. & Maurin, A. (2012) An Analysis of Economic Cycles of the English Speaking Caribbean Countries. Mimeo.

http://www.cbvs.sr/CCMF/ccmf_papers/Economic%20cycles%20of%20the%20English%20speaking%20Caribbean_Craigwell%20&%20Wright.pdf

Dickens, W.T. & Madrick, J.G (2010) Long-term Consequences of Economic Fluctuations. Mimeo

Du Plessis, Stan (2006) Business Cycles in Emerging Market Economies: A new View of the Stylized Facts. Stellenbosch Economic Working Papers: 2/ 2006.

Dutt, Amitava Krishna, & Ros, Jaime, (2009). Long-run effects of aggregate demand fluctuations. Preliminary draft. Prepared for a Schwartz Center for Economic Policy Analysis conference on "The Long Term Impacts of Short Term Fluctuations: Theory, Evidence and Policy" at the Brookings Institution, November 5-6, 2009.

ECLAC (2002). Globalization and Development. ECLAC. Santiago, Chile.

ECLAC (2012). Structural change for Equality. ECLAC: Santiago, Chile.

European Commission (2009) Impact of the current economic and financial crisis on potential output. Occasional Papers No. 49. Directorate-General for Economic and Financial Affairs http://ec.europa.eu/economy_finance/publications

Frisch, R. (1933) Propagation problems and impuls problems in dynamic economics, in Economic essays in honour of Gustav Cassel, London, George Allen and Unwin Ltd.., 171-205.

Harding, Don and Pagan, Adrian (2002a). "A comparison of two business cycle dating methods." Journal of Economic Dynamics and Control 27: 1681-1690.

Harding, Don and Pagan, Adrian (2002b). "Dissecting the cycle: a methodological investigation." Journal of Monetary Economics 49: 365-381.

Harding, Don and Pagan, Adrian (2002c). "Rejoinder to James Hamilton." Journal of Economic Dynamics and Control 27: 1695-1698.

Harding, Don and Pagan, Adrian (2005). "A suggested framework for classifying the modes of cycle research." Journal of applied econometrics 20(2): 151-159.IMF (2009) World Economic Outlook. Washington D.C. : IMF

Kydland, F.E. & Prescott, E.C. (1990) Business Cycles: Real Facts and a Monetary Myth. Federal Reserve Bank of Minnesota Quarterly Review, Spring, 383-398.

Lucas, R. (1987) Models of Business Cycles. Oxfrod: Basil Blackwell

Male, Rachel Louise (2009) Developing Country Business Cycles: Characterizing the Cycle and Investigating the Output Persistence Problem. PhD Thesis. University of York. Department of Economics and Related Studies.

Medio, A. "trade cycle." The New Palgrave Dictionary of Economics. Second Edition. Eds. Steven N. Durlauf and Lawrence E. Blume. Palgrave Macmillan, 2008. The New Palgrave Dictionary of Economics Online. Palgrave Macmillan. 28 January 2013

http://www.dictionaryofeconomics.com/article?

Pagan, A. (2003) Three Views of the Business Cycles and their Implications. Mimeo. Lecture given at SMU.

Pérez Caldentey, E. & Pineda R. (2011) Does Latin America lag behind due to shaper recessions and/or slower recoveries? MPRA Working Paper 25036,University Library of Munich, Germany http://mpra.ub.uni-muenchen.de/25036/

Ramey, Garey & Ramey, Valerie A, (1995). "Cross-Country Evidence on the Link between Volatility and Growth," American Economic Review, American Economic Association, vol. 85(5), pages 1138-51, December.

Rand, J., and Tarp, F. (2002) "Business Cycles in Developing Countries: Are They Different?" World Development 30(12); pp.2071-2088.

Sargent, Th.J. (1987) Macroeconomic Theory, 2nd edition. Boston:Academic Press.

Titelman, D., Pérez Caldentey, E. and Carvallo, P. (2011) The stylized facts of the Latin American and Caribbean Business Cycle. ECLAC. Mimeo.

Titelman, D., E. Pérez-Caldentey and R. Minzer (2008), "Una comparación de la dinámica e impactos de los choques de términos de intercambio y financieros en América Latina 1980-2006", Serie FInanciamiento del Desarrollo. Santiago, Chile, Economic Commission for Latin America and the Caribbean (ECLAC).

Turnovsky S. & Chattopadhyay, P, (1998) "Volatility and Growth in Developing Economies: Some Numerical Results and Empirical Evidence," Discussion Papers in Economics at the University of Washington 0055, Department of Economics at the University of Washington.

World Bank (2013) World Development Indicators and Global Finance. Wahington D.C. http://databank.worldbank.org/ddp/home.do?Step=2&id=4&DisplayAggregation=N&SdmxSupporte d=Y&CNO=2&SET_BRANDING=YES

Yigit, F.P. (2004) Re-evaluating the link between volatility and growth (2003) Electronic Theses, Treatises and Dissertations. Paper 664.

Zambelli, S. (2007). A Rocking Horse That Never Rocked: Frisch's "Propagation Problems and Impulse Problems, History of Political Economy, Duke University Press, vol. 39(1), pages 145-166, Spring.

Zarnowitz, V (1992) "Macroeconomics and Business Cycles: An Overview," NBER Chapters, in: Business Cycles: Theory, History, Indicators, and Forecasting, pages 1-19 National Bureau of Economic Research, Inc.

Appendix: list of countries included and respective time domain for GDP

	First observation	Last observation
East Asia and Pacific		
China	1993:Q1	2012:Q1
Indonesia	1997:Q1	2012:Q2
Malaysia	1989:Q1	2012:Q1
Filipinas	1989:Q1	2011:Q4
Thailand	1993:Q1	2012:Q1
Europe and Central Asia		
Bulgaria	2002:Q1	2011:Q4
Belorussia	1992:Q1	2012:Q1
Georgia	1996:Q1	2011:Q4
Kyrgyzstan	2000:Q1	2012:Q1
Latvia	1990:Q1	2012:Q1
Lithuania	1993:Q1	2012:Q1
Rumania	1998:Q1	2012:Q1
Russia	1995:Q1	2012:Q1
Turkey	1989:Q1	2012:Q1
Ukraine	2001:Q1	2012:Q1
Macedonia, FYR	2004:Q1	2012:Q1
Latin America and the Caribbean		
Argentina	1990:Q1	2012:Q2
Bolivia	1990:Q1	2012:Q1
Brazil	1990:Q1	2012:Q2
Belize	2000:Q1	2012:Q1
Chile	1989:Q1	2012:Q1
Colombia	1994:Q1	2011:Q4
Costa Rica	1991:Q1	2012:Q1
Dominican Rep.	1992:Q1	2012:Q1
Ecuador	1990:Q1	2012:Q1
El Salvador	1990:Q1	2012:Q1
Guatemala	2001:Q1	2012:Q1
Grenada	2000:Q1	2012:Q2
Jamaica	1996:Q1	2012:Q1
Mexico	1990:Q1	2012:Q2
Nicaragua	1994:Q1	2012:Q1
Panama	1996:Q1	2012:Q1
Paraguay	1994:Q1	2012:Q1
Peru	1989:Q1	2012:Q2
Saint Lucia	2000:Q1	2012:Q2
Uruguay	1997:Q1	2012:Q2
Venezuela	1993:Q1	2012:Q2
Middle East and North Africa		
Jordan	1992:Q1	2011:Q4
Morocco	1990:Q1	2011:Q4
Tunisia	2000:Q1	2010:Q4

South Asia		
India	1996:Q4	2011:Q4
Sub-Saharan Africa		
Botswana	1994:Q1	2011:Q4
Mauricio	2000:Q1	2012:Q1
South Africa	1989:Q1	2012:Q2
High Income		
Australia	1989:Q1	2012:Q2
Austria	1989:Q1	2012:Q1
Barbados	1990:Q1	2012:Q2
Belgium	1989:Q1	2012:Q1
Brunei	2003:Q1	2011:Q4
Canada	1989:Q1	2012:Q2
Croatia	1993:Q1	2012:Q1
Cyprus	1995:Q1	2012:Q1
Czech Republic	1994:Q1	2012:Q1
Denmark	1989:Q1	2012:Q1
Estonia	1993:Q1	2012:Q1
Finland	1989:Q1	2011:Q4
France	1989:Q1	2012:Q2
Germany	1989:Q1	2012:Q2
Hong Kong	1989:Q1	2012:Q1
Hungary	1995:Q1	2012:Q1
Ireland	1997:Q1	2012:Q2
Island	1997:Q1	2012:Q2
Israel	1989:Q1	2012:Q2
Italy	1989:Q1	2012:Q2
Japan	1989:Q1	2012:Q2
Luxemburg	1995:Q1	2012:Q1
Macao	1998:Q1	2012:Q1
Malta	1996:Q1	2011:Q4
Netherlands	1989:Q1	2012:Q2
New Zealand	1989:Q1	2012:Q2
Norway	1989:Q1	2012:Q1
Poland	1995:Q1	2012:Q1
Portugal	1989:Q1	2011:Q4
Rep. of Korea	1989:Q1	2012:Q1
Singapore	1989:Q1	2011:Q4
Slovakia	1993:Q1	2012:Q1
Slovenia	1992:Q1	2012:Q1
Spain	1989:Q1	2012:Q2
Sweden	1989:Q1	2012:Q1
Switzerland	1989:Q1	2012:Q1
Trinidad and Tobago	2000:Q1	2012:Q1
United Kingdom	1989:Q1	2012:Q2
United States	1989:Q1	2012:Q2

Macro Policies For Climate Change: Free Market Or State Intervention?

Pablo Ruiz Nápoles[1]
Economics Department, Universidad Nacional Autónoma de México, Mexico

Abstract

The central issue studied in this essay is the meaning and implications for public policy of Nicholas Stern's statement that "Climate change is the greatest and widest-ranging *market failure* ever seen" (Stern, 2006).

To deal with this issue we analyze the two big currents about public policy measures in general: market oriented and state intervention. We also present the current conceptual framework for debating public policy for analyzing the policies recommended and applied so far, to deal with Climate Change's causes and effects, from an economic perspective. We present the main arguments of the Stern Review. Finally we get into the debate between Stern and Nordhaus. Our conclusion is that there is a need for *strong state intervention* to make the climate change mitigation policies to reach the desired effects.

Keywords: market failure, public policy, climate change, welfare.

JEL: H23 Q54, Q58

Introduction

On July 2005, in the United Kingdom an independent Review was commissioned, by the Chancellor of the Exchequer, reporting to both the Chancellor and to the Prime Minister, as a contribution to assessing the evidence and building understanding of the economics of climate change. The Review was commissioned to Nicholas Stern. The Review examined the evidence on the economic impacts of climate change itself, and explored the economics of stabilizing greenhouse gases in the atmosphere (Stern, 2006, 2007).

Stern states in the summary that: "Climate change presents a unique challenge for economics: it is the greatest and widest-ranging *market failure* ever seen" (Stern,

---

[1] Author contact: ruizna@unam.mx

2006). What did Stern mean by this statement and what were its implications for public policy regarding climate change?

This is the main question we are addressing in this essay. For that purpose, in the first section we briefly analyze the two big currents about public policy measures in general: market oriented or state intervention and we present the current conceptual framework for debating public policy. In the second section, we analyze the policies recommended and applied so far, to deal with Climate Change's causes and effects, from an economic perspective. In the third section, the main findings of Stern Review are presented. The fourth section deals with the Nordhaus versus Stern debate. Finally, some conclusions are drawn.

I. The political Economy debate: free market *versus* state intervention

There has always been in Political Economy a paradigmatic division among those who favor state intervention in designing and applying economic policy (the interventionists) and those who do not favor the state intervention in the economy at all (the liberals). The debate, as old as the capitalist economy itself, has involved all types of issues. Some of these issues are purely ideological, some are theoretical, but all involve the design and implementation of public policies aimed to improving the economic well-being of the population, to fostering economic development and/or to preventing economic crises.

The state intervention argument has its origin in the early stage of capitalism in England, commercial capitalism, whose theorists, like Misselden and Mun, defended protectionist policies and monopoly's concessions granted by the state, in the sixteenth and seventeenth centuries All of this was strongly opposed by the liberals Petty, Locke, North, Law, Hume and Smith, in the seventeenth and eighteenth centuries, who favored free trade and no state intervention in the economy (see Schumpeter, 1966, and Roll, 1974). The debate was apparently won by the liberals whose theories dominated the economic thinking at the time. In practice, however, during the nineteenth century except for Britain, not one of today developed European countries, or the United States, followed free trade policies but, quite the contrary, all of their governments protected their local industries against foreign competition as a strategy for development, leaded by the state (see Chang, 2002).

The debate was reopened in the twentieth century mostly due to the 1930s deep crisis of the US economy and, in particular, the remedies followed for recovering. So, in the second a quarter of the past century the debate was leaded, on the interventionist side by the British John M., Keynes, and on the liberal side by the Austrian Friedrich A., von Hayek (see Foley, 2006). There was a period in which Keynesianism seemed to prevail. But in the last fifty years Neoclassical thinking, labeled also as *neoliberal* has been predominant within the so called *Mainstream Economics* – the accepted paradigm in Economics – both in theory, that is, teaching, and in practice, that is, policy, in most capitalist countries. So much so, that Keynes' analysis was adopted by Samuelson and Hicks, both prominent neoclassicals, as a constituent part of accepted theory (mainstream economics) in what Joan Robinson defined as "Bastard Keynesianism" (Robinson, 1962).

Most recently the protection of the environment has been one of the issues under debate between these two main currents (interventionist and liberals). There have been those who favor state intervention on environmental matters from an extreme called *nationalized delivery* of environmental protection, and those who rely on the free market mechanism (Adam Smith's *Invisible Hand*) to self-regulating the, potentially dangerous to the environment, activities. There has been, of course, also a wide space for a variety of policies in between the two extremes (see Hepburn, 2010, pp.121-122). Hepburn says that unlike many areas of economic activity, for the environment relying on the free market is highly unlikely to deliver satisfactory outcomes because firms have inadequate incentives to internalize externalities without government intervention. On the other extreme, state provision is said to entail a great politicization of operational decisions (and hence a low economic efficiency) and may require a great deal of information which is often unavailable. So, he says the impossibility of a free market approach and the inefficiency of nationalized delivery, imply a role for government in the middle of the spectrum (Hepburn, 2010).

The conceptual framework of the debate has been based on the neoclassical Utility theory at social level, *i.e.*, modern Welfare Economics, developed since the late thirties by, among others, Bergson (1938), Arrow (1951) and Debreu (1954). A crucial aspect of this theory, *i.e.* the interpersonal comparisons of utility, was challenged by Nicholas Kaldor (1938) and defended by Lionel Robbins (1938), with a no definitive result.

Within this conceptual framework a *market failure* is a situation where in the allocation of resources by a free market is not efficient. That is, there exists another conceivable outcome where a market participant may be made better-off without making someone else worse-off. A market failure can be viewed as a scenario where individuals' pursuit of pure self-interest leads to an outcome that is not Pareto efficient. An economic system that is not Pareto efficient implies that a certain change in allocation of goods may result in some individuals being made "better off" with no individual being made worse off, and therefore can be made more Pareto efficient through a Pareto improvement. Here "better off" is interpreted as "put in a preferred position." It is commonly accepted that outcomes that are not Pareto efficient are to be avoided, and therefore Pareto efficiency becomes an important criterion for evaluating economic systems and public policies. If a market failure exists, mainstream – both neoclassical and Keynesian – economists believe that it may be possible for a government to improve the inefficient market outcome, while several heterodox schools of thought disagree with this.

Different economists have different views about what events are the sources of a market failure. Joseph Stiglitz points out that, early discussions of market failure, like the one of Bator (1958) focused on externalities, natural monopolies, and public goods. Later discussions focused on problems of incomplete markets, imperfect information, and the pervasiveness of imperfect competition (Stiglitz, 1991) all of which are analyzed by Stiglitz himself.

But what about unequal income distribution as resulting of free market operation, is it a market failure? Stiglitz says that, according to the second fundamental theorem of welfare economics, we can separate out issues of economic efficiency from issues of equity. But as it turns out, in his analysis of the second theorem and some cases of imperfect markets, we cannot (Stiglitz, 1991, p. 28 and p. 30).

Stiglitz finds that since the mid-60s, there has been "a closer examination of Adam Smith's invisible hand. The theoretical research has taken two different strands (reflecting two ideological strands within the profession). The first has attempted to show that the economy is Pareto efficient under much more general conditions than those originally used by Arrow and Debreu. The second has attempted to show that there were assumptions in Arrow and Debreu's analysis which, while perhaps mentioned, did not receive the attention they deserved. These assumptions make the theorems [of welfare] of limited relevance to modern industrial economies. In this view, Adam Smith's invisible hand may be invisible because, like the Emperor's new clothes, it simply isn't there; or if it is there, it is too palsied to be relied upon" (Stiglitz, 1991, p.5). The two schools are thus defined as Microeconomics and Macroeconomics, and the crucial discrepancy between them is related to the explanation of unemployment in capitalist economies, while for the first it is a temporary and not significant phenomenon, for the second it is endemic to the capitalist system and shows the irrelevance of welfare economics and perfect competition theorems (Stiglitz, 1991, p.7).

To these, another source of market failure has been added: the question of incentives or principal-agent problems. The Theory of Incentives or Principal-agent models (Laffont and Martimort, 2002) is the most recent development within the neoclassical anti-interventionist approach, according to Chang (2003, p. 27). In his opinion these models are usually presented as neutral efficiency arguments but have much deeper political impacts.

The Principal-Agent approach has inspired market oriented environmental policies for various areas of concern (see for example, Franckx and D'Amato, 2009; Szatzschneider and Kwiatkowska, 2008). In the case of Climate Change mitigation policies, the Principal - Agent theory is at the base of the "Carbon markets" policy, aimed mainly to incentive producers, which are high GHG emitters, to switch from high carbon technologies to low carbon technologies, *i.e.* the so called "Cap-and-Trade" policy. The model is also oriented to consumers (see Schatzki T. and R.N. Stavins, 2012). In either case, it has very strong limitations in practice (see Ackerman, 2008). But also in theory, it is well known the "Principal-Agent problem".[2] Stiglitz shows that all principal-agent problems are not Pareto efficient, therefore, they are market failures as well (Stiglitz, 1991, p. 30).

In sum, we may say that the basic criterion to define what is, and what is not, a *market failure* depends entirely on considerations of efficiency as defined by modern welfare economics, completely dominated by neoclassical thinking. However, in practice there has been some room for the application of protectionist (non-efficient) policies or other interventionists (*i.e.* non-free market) measures, considered as *second-best* policies, when the first-best policy is "regarded as politically or institutionally impossible" (Kindleberger, 1973, p.200). If *free market*, as an institution, is not working, then there is

---

[2] Principal-agent problem is a particular game-theoretic description of a situation. There is a player called a principal, and one or more other players called agents with utility functions that are in some sense different from the principal's. The principal can act more effectively through the agents than directly, and must construct incentive schemes to get them to behave at least partly according to the principal's interests. The principal-agent problem is that of designing the incentive scheme. The actions of the agents may not be observable so it is not usually sufficient for the principal just to condition payment on the actions of the agents.
http://economics.about.com/od/economicsglossary/g/principalag.htm.

a market failure, and so it is justified the use of interventionist measures, as a second best policy, even within the neoclassical tradition.

II. The environment as subject of public policy

Widespread social awareness about the environment being endangered by pollution, produced by human activities, started in the sixties. This was mainly due to scientific discoveries about the occurrence of this phenomenon and its magnitude, affecting various natural habitats of animal and plants, all over the world. However, pollution was seen then as a local, *i.e.* national, or a regional, problem, concerning therefore local governments to deal with it or reaching regional agreements to the same purpose. Moreover, since stopping or preventing pollution implied reducing the levels of production and consumption in the short run, affecting in principle the economy of a given country and its population, it was a matter seen as concerning first the national producers and consumers and, therefore, national authorities, that is, the *state*, as the representative of the nation.

Accordingly public policies aimed to reduce or eliminate pollution were carried out by the state through the usual means of state intervention in the economy, *i.e.*, fixation of rules and standards for pollution activities, like time or space limits, technology improvements, and various types of economic and or legal sanctions against violators of these rules; taxes were also included and even prohibitions in the use or production of polluting substances, or their free disposal to the air, water or land.

Still, one of the main contributors to earth pollution (rivers, seas, lands and, specially, air), which is *oil*, could not be banned, neither in its production, nor in its use as the main fuel for industrial activities in and for consumption. In other words, all economies in the world depended, one way or another, on oil fuels and alternative technologies were not technically or economically feasible in most countries. A few countries, however, developed nuclear facilities for non-military purposes, looking for the substitution of fuel power by nuclear power, mainly to produce electricity.

Everything changed in the eighties in Environmental Economics. On the one hand, there was a boom in world trade in goods and capitals, as a result of the opening of many local and regional markets previously closed by protectionist practices, which was baptized as *globalization*. It showed the actual predominance of *Neoliberalism* inspiring free market economic policies in most developed countries and in many developing ones as well. On the other, there was the scientific confirmation of an old hypothesis regarding a great environmental phenomenon, this one affecting the whole planet: Global Warming.

II.i Neoliberalism of the eighties

Hepburn says that during the 1970s the state kept on growing in many developed countries as a result of the Keynesian public programs and policies tendencies from the past, but the revival of monetarist theory began to provide growing intellectual opposition to increasing enlargement and more important growth faltered in the 1970's with the oil shocks and the collapse of the Bretton Woods system. These conditions ushered Margaret Thatcher into power in the UK, in 1979, and Ronald Regan in the US, in 1980, with a corresponding change in political philosophy. In due course this would also change the environmental policy with the creation of "environmental markets" (Hepburn, 2010).

Global warming and climate change

In 1985 a joint the United Nations Environment Program (UNEP) and the World Meteorological Organization (WMO) Conference on the "Assessment of the Role of Carbon Dioxide and Other Greenhouse Gases in Climate Variations and Associated Impacts" assessed the role of carbon dioxide and aerosols in the atmosphere, and concluded that greenhouse gases "are expected" to cause significant warming in the next century and that some warming was inevitable (WMO, 1986). In June 1988, James E. Hansen made one of the first assessments that human-caused warming had already measurably affected global climate (Hansen, 1988).

Accordingly, the Intergovernmental Panel on Climate Change (IPCC) was created in 1988, under the United Nations and the World Meteorological Organization. Since then, the IPCC has tried to induce state and public policies' options for adaptation and mitigation of Climate Change (IPCC, 2011). And given that Climate change is a global phenomenon in its causes and in its effects, it required a political platform among countries to cope with it. So, the IPCC played a decisive role in the creation of the United Nations Framework Convention on Climate Change (UNFCCC) in 1990, and the adoption of the Kyoto Protocol in 1997.

II.ii Policy recommendations of the IPCC and the OECD

The measures originally suggested by IPCC for adaptation and mitigation of Climate Change were grouped into five categories: market based programs; regulatory measures; voluntary agreements; scientific research and development (R&D); and infrastructural measures. The IPCC clearly warned that: "No single measure will be sufficient for the timely development, adoption and diffusion of the mitigation options. Rather, a combination of measures adapted to national, regional and local conditions will be required" (IPCC, 1996).

Five years later, the 2001 IPCC Report on Mitigation pointed out that, important considerations in the analysis of climate change mitigation options are, differences in the distribution of technological, natural and financial resources among and within nations and regions, and between generations, as well as differences in mitigation costs. And – it said – there is also an important issue of *equity*, namely the extent to which the impacts of climate change or mitigation policies create or exacerbate inequities both within and across nations and regions. It said too that the various estimates of cost and benefits of mitigation actions differ because of how welfare is measured, the scope and methodology of the analysis, and the underlying assumptions built into the analysis. As a result, it says, estimated costs and benefits may not reflect the actual costs and benefits of implementing mitigation actions (IPCC, 2001). With respect to mitigation policies the report recommended that "national responses to climate change can be more effective if deployed as a portfolio of policy instruments to limit or reduce greenhouse gas emissions...[which]... may include emissions-carbon-energy taxes, tradable or non-tradable permits, provision and/or removal of subsidies, deposit-refund systems, technology or performance standards, energy mix requirements, product bans, voluntary agreements, government spending and investment, and support for research and development." Some report's findings on this matter are that "Energy efficiency standards and performance regulations are widely used, and may be effective in many countries, and sometimes precede market based instruments. Voluntary agreements have been used more frequently, sometimes preceding the introduction of more stringent measures. Information campaigns, environmental labeling, and green marketing, alone or in combination with incentive subsidies, are increasingly emphasized to inform and shape consumer or producer behavior" (IPCC, 2001).

In these reports the need for state intervention arises also from the existence of *market imperfections* in each and every economy in the world. The OECD emphasizes that putting a price on GHG emissions, through price mechanisms, has the limitation that "they do not address the full range of *market imperfections* that prevent emissions to be cut at least cost, such as information problems" (Duval, 2008).

The OECD finds also that empirical analysis indicates that the most important determinant of innovation in the area of renewable energy technologies is general innovative capacity. However – the OECD study says – in the case of energy "public policy makes a difference. Public R&D expenditures on renewable energies induce innovation, as do targeted measures such as renewable energy certificates and feed-in tariffs" (Haščič, et al., 2010).

Finally, another issue that calls for state action is the "issue of equity, namely the extent to which the impacts of climate change or mitigation policies create or exacerbate inequities both within and across nations and regions". This implies the need for the application of state policy measures aiming to prevent or to compensate any inequities that may result from either climate change impacts or mitigation policies, between sectors or population groups within a country, and internationally agreed regulations in the same direction for inequities between countries.

Despite all recommendations, market oriented policies prevailed in most countries and they did help, but little, in solving the GHG emissions problem. So, Nicholas Stern pointed out in his Review in 2006, after eighteen years of the IPCC foundation, that Climate Change was "…the greatest and widest-ranging *market failure* ever seen" (Stern, 2006). Stern also called for a "major change" (as opposed to a marginal one) in GHG reductions.

Now, we can interpret more clearly what he meant by "market failure". In the first place this is a situation – as defined above – in which free market yields an outcome which is not Pareto efficient. The reasons for that may be, as IPCC and OECD pointed out the existence of market imperfections in most countries; that we are dealing with a negative externality that cannot be internalized by firms without government intervention, according to Hepburn's opinion; that pollution is a public good, or rather a *public bad*, and therefore its price cannot be determined by free market forces; that it is a case of *imperfect information* as the OECD pointed out (Duval, 2008); or finally as Hepburn based on Stiglitz considers, that this a market failure due to principal-agent problems (Hepburn, 2010: Stiglitz, 1991). For all these reasons, there seems to be no doubt that

Climate Change is a great market failure, even within the neoclassical welfare economics analysis framework. But there is also another cause of market failure that applies in this case, the question of *equity*, emphasized by IPCC and OECD, whether or not this cause is considered a valid one in modern welfare economics.

Therefore this great market failure calls for *state intervention*, even as a second best policy, that is, with full awareness that it is not possible to have a Pareto efficient solution, in modern welfare economics terms. And this state intervention has to be as large as the size of the problem to be solved, in order to produce the *major change* it is required, as Stern stated.

According to Hepburn (2010 p.121-122): "The degree of state involvement in delivering social outcomes (such as environmental protection) might be considered to be on a spectrum running from 'free market' at one end, to 'nationalized delivery' at the other end:

- Free market: no government involvement; individuals and firms voluntarily acquire information on externalities and voluntarily and altruistically internalize those externalities;

- Information provision: government assumes the role of aggregating and disseminating information about externalities and their shadow prices, but does nothing more;

- Moral suasion: government provides information and may even seek to persuade people and firms to change their preferences and objectives. In its best form, this might constitute a form of 'government by discussion';

- Economy-wide relative prices: government determines the appropriate price or quantity of the social good or externality (e.g. carbon dioxide CO_2) emissions, SO_2 emissions, water effluent, biodiversity) and implements policy to correct relative prices (e.g. economy-wide taxes, trading schemes, etc.);

- Output-based intervention: government specifies output standards for specific sectors or firms (e.g. CO_2/MW standards), but does not require the use of any particular method to deliver those standards;

- Input – or technology – based intervention: government specifies or encourages or requires firms to employ particular technologies or inputs (e.g. SO2 scrubbers), either through explicit regulation or through taxes or subsidies;

144

- Project-level intervention: government specifies or encourages particular projects to occur, through subsidy or other financial (e.g. balance sheet) support (e.g. EU carbon capture and storage (CCS) program);
- State capitalism: state-owned enterprises follow guidance given by their (government) shareholder; some flexibility for implementation may be retained if targets are expressed and political incentives put in place, but often executives are given direct instructions;
- Nationalized delivery: government finances and delivers on environmental protection directly through central government departments".

These types of policy measures with the exception of the first three require some degree of state intervention. The first four – mostly market oriented – are the most popular and have been tried even together in various countries aiming to the same target: reducing GHG emissions, but the results so far have not been fully satisfactory. While GHG emissions have been effectively reduced in some countries, they have not in others and the global level of emissions keeps growing dangerously. As Stern himself pointed out, Climate Change is a "Global" problem and requires "Global" measures to face it, that is, general agreements among all countries (involving especially those which are the higher GHG emitters) applying the same policy measures to reduce emissions.

II.iii Policies results 1990-2010

Table 1 shows that most parties in the so called 42 parties of Annex I of the United Nations Framework Convention on Climate Change (UNFCCC), with the exception of the United States, have reduced to some extent their GHG emissions (mostly motivated by the Kyoto Protocol signed in 1997) which implied the use of some sort of state enforced *regulations*, which, according to Nordhaus (2007b), represents the alternative (inefficient) policy to his most favored market oriented policy, *i.e.*, carbon taxes, in this case called harmonized carbon tax (HCT) policy, using only the price mechanism to reduce GHG emissions.

Table 1 Greenhouse gas (GHG) emissions: selected years in Gg CO_2 equivalent (in millions)

	1990	1994	1995	1996	2000	2005	2009	2010	2011	Per cent variation 2010/ 1990
All countries	22.47	22.98	23.46	23.99	24.81	29.68	32.05	33.62		49.6
Annex I countries	17.69	15.84	16.07	16.03	16.06	16.15	14.76	15.42	15.28	-12.9
United States	5.39	5.64	5.76	5.95	6.39	6.20	5.55	5.75	5.80	6.7
European Union (27)	5.32	4.87	4.92	5.02	4.79	4.86	4.27	4.41	4.26	-17.1
Russian Federation	3.44	2.11	1.98	1.84	1.59	1.59	1.46	1.56	1.69	-54.7
Japan	1.20	1.28	1.26	1.27	1.26	1.26	1.13	1.18	1.23	-1.3
Non-Annex I countries	4.77	7.13	7.39	7.96	8.75	13.53	17.29	18.20		281.2
China	n.d.	3.65	n.d.	n.d.	n.d.	7.05	n.d.	7.83	n.d.	
India	n.d.	1.23	n.d.	n.d.	1.30	n.d.	n.d.	1.90	n.d.	
Other countries	n.d.	2.26	n.d.	n.d.	n.d.	n.d.	n.d.	n.d.	n.d.	

Sources: Elaborated with data from UNFCCC Data Interface except for data in italics taken from Tom Boden and Bob Andres, Carbon Dioxide Information Analysis Center Oak Ridge National Laboratory and Gregg Marland, Research Institute for Environmental, Energy and Economics Appalachian State University

Given these tendencies the OECD projected the scenario for 2050 shown in Figure 1 below, where it is clear that the only mitigation policy working simultaneously all over the world is that of increasing CO_2 sinks, which means reducing and recovering deforestation.

It must be noted that figures for total GHG emissions for the year 2010 do not coincide with those from UNFCCC due to various methodological differences. However, the important question is that most mitigation policies applied in some countries have a reduced effect in the overall GHG emissions tendencies, mainly due to those countries which are not regulating enough their emissions or not regulating at all, and they happen to be the most important GHG emissions producers.

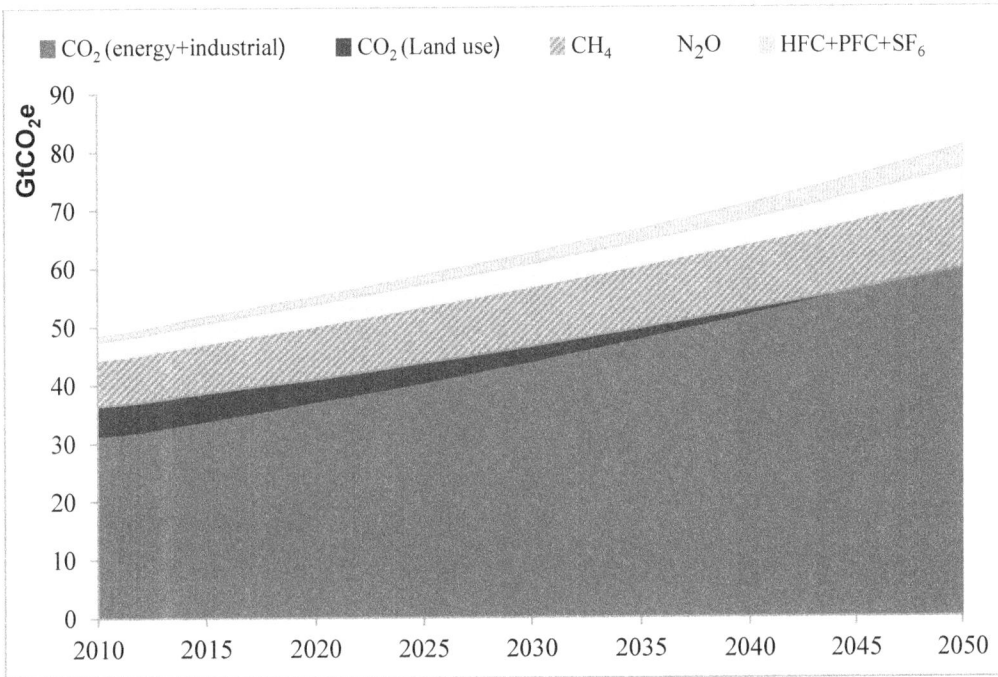

Figure 1 GHG emissions: *Baseline,* 2010-2050 Panel by gases

Source: OECD Environmental Outlook Baseline

III. The Stern Review

The Stern Review (2006) was published sixteen years after the *IPCC First Assessment Report* (1990) and ten years after the *IPCC Technical Report* (1996).

From the very beginning Stern makes a very strong statement: "The scientific evidence is now overwhelming, climate change presents very serious global risks, and it demands an urgent global response". Almost immediately Stern introduces the famous paragraph: "Climate change presents a unique challenge for economics: it is the greatest and widest-ranging market failure ever seen. The economic analysis must, therefore, be global, deal with long time horizons, have the economics of risk and uncertainty at center stage, and examine the possibility of major, non-marginal change".

The Stern Review consists basically of three assessments: (1) an analysis of the GHG emissions tendencies and their effects on climate change in particular, the increase of earth's mean temperature (global warming); (2) an estimation of the probable impacts (mostly negative) of this global warming on economic and social life, all over the world, in monetary terms, including non-market damages and, (3) a series of recommendations for policy measures aimed directly to reduce GHG emissions, in order to stabilize CO_2 concentrations in the atmosphere, before a critical level is reached.

Figure A Historical and projected GHG emissions by sector (by source)

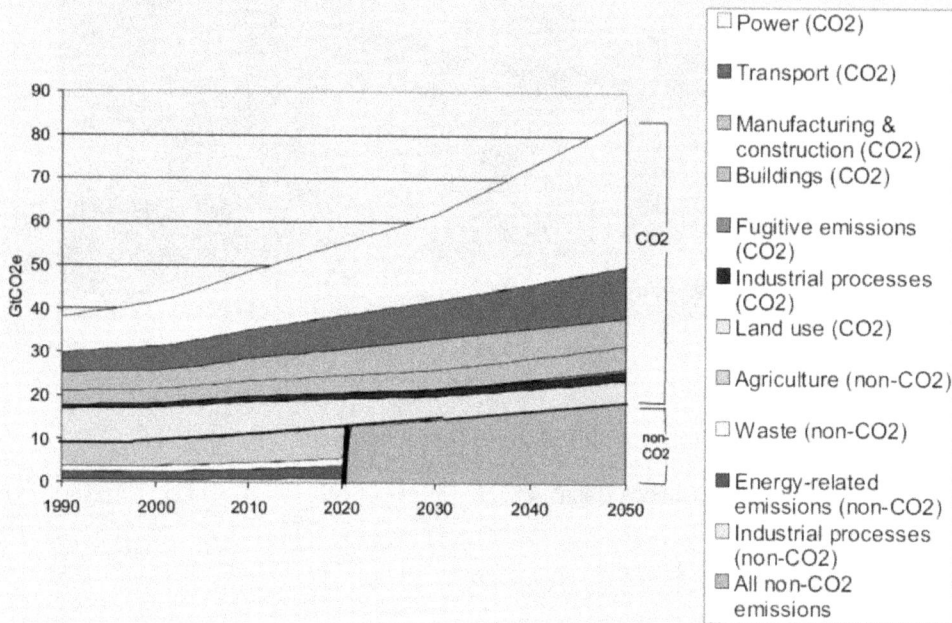

Figure 2
Source: Stern Review: The Economics of Climate Change, p. 173.

III.i GHG emissions under "business as usual" (BAU)

At the time of the Stern Review, the level of GHG concentration in the atmosphere was estimated of around 430 parts per million (ppm), CO_2 equivalent, compared with 280ppm before the Industrial Revolution, *i.e.*, 1750-1850. Given the estimated annual rate of GHG emissions flow for 2005, the first prediction of the Stern Review was that if this flow of emissions would not increase at a higher rate than this, the concentration of GHG in the atmosphere would reach *double* pre-industrial levels by 2050 (550ppm CO_2 eq.). But, the annual flow of GHG emissions was already accelerating, so the level of 550ppm CO_2 eq. could be reached earlier, by 2035. At this level the Review says there is *at least* a 77 per cent chance of a global average temperature rise *exceeding* 2°C. And under a "business as usual" (BAU) scenario the stock of GHG could *more than triple* by 2100, with at least a 50 per cent risk of exceeding 5°C global average temperature change during the following decades. "This would – the Review warns – take humans into *unknown territory*" (Stern, 2006, pp. iv and 158).

III.ii Climate change damages and costs

The Review considers three approaches for estimating the costs of climate change:

Estimating physical impacts on economic activity, on human life and on the environment

The Stern prediction based on scientific models is that under a BAU scenario, average global temperatures will rise by 2-3°C within the next fifty years. But if GHG emissions continue to grow the Earth will be subject to several degrees more warming. However, this predicted situation will not be the same for all countries, since the impacts of climate change are not evenly distributed, that is, the poorest countries will be the most affected and the earliest. On the other hand, while climate change may have small positive effects for a few developed countries in the beginning, it is likely to be very damaging for higher temperature increases. The *costs* of extreme weather alone could reach 0.5 to 1 per cent of world GDP per year by 2050, and will keep rising if the world continues to warm.

Estimating monetary aggregates of costs and risks with the use of IAMs

This approach implies the use of Integrated Assessment Models (IAMs) that produce aggregate monetary estimates of costs. Again a strong statement by Stern was: "The monetary impacts of climate change are now expected to be more serious than many earlier studies suggested, not least because those studies tended to exclude some of the most uncertain but potentially most damaging impacts" (Stern, 2006, p. viii).

Stern argues that formal IAMs in the past used as a starting point a scenario of 2 to 3°C warming and in this temperature range the cost of climate change could be equivalent to a permanent average loss of 0 to 3 per cent in global world output. But, given the uneven distribution of damages, developing countries will suffer even higher costs. However – he says – more recent evidence indicates that temperature changes resulting from BAU trends in GHG emissions may exceed 2–3°C by the end of this century. And, this increases the likelihood of a wider range of impacts than previously considered. Moreover, many of these impacts are more difficult to quantify. With 5-6°C warming, existing models that include the risk of abrupt and large-scale climate change estimate an average of 5-10 per cent loss in global GDP, with poor countries suffering costs above 10 per cent of GDP.

The Review uses one particular model PAGE 2002 – that includes the possibility to analyze risks explicitly – in order to analyze the response of these models to updated scientific evidence on the probabilities attached to degrees of temperature rise. Besides the using of the model with one set of data consistent with the climate predictions of the 2001 IPCC Report, it was also utilized with another set of data that includes a small increase in the amplifying feedbacks in the climate system. The model also considered "how the application of appropriate discount rates, assumptions about the equity weighting attached to the valuation of impacts in poor countries, and estimates of the impacts on mortality and the environment would increase the estimated economic costs of climate change"[3] (Stern, 2006, p. ix). The Stern's model estimated the total cost over the next two centuries of climate change associated under BAU, GHG emissions of an equivalent to an average reduction in global per-capita consumption of at least 5 per cent.

But – Stern goes on – the cost of climate change impacts under a BAU path would increase still further, if the model takes into account three important factors: (1) including direct impacts on the environment and human health (called 'non-market' impacts), increases the total cost of climate change from 5 per cent to 11 per cent of global per-capita consumption; (2) recent scientific evidence indicates that the climate system may be more responsive to GHG emissions than previously thought, because of the existence of amplifying feedbacks. Stern estimates that the potential scale of the climate response could increase the cost of climate change on the BAU path from 5 to 7 per cent of global consumption, or from 11 to 14 per cent, if the non-market impacts are included; (3) a disproportionate share of the climate-change burden falls on poor regions of the world; when this unequal burden is weighted appropriately, the estimated global cost of climate change at 5-6°C warming could be more than 25 per cent higher than without such weights.

---

[3] There is a complete section in the Stern Review for the discussion of the "discount rate" (see Stern, 2006 pp.31-32).

So, putting these additional factors together would increase the total cost of BAU climate change to the equivalent of around a 20 per cent reduction in consumption per head, now and into the future. In sum, analyses that take into account the full ranges of both impacts and possible outcomes suggest that BAU climate change will reduce welfare by an amount equivalent to a reduction in consumption per head of between 5 and 20 per cent.

Comparing costs and benefits of action

This approach compares estimates of the changes in the expected benefits and costs over time from a little extra reduction in emissions, and avoids large-scale formal economic models.

According to the Review calculations, the social cost of carbon, on a BAU trajectory, was about $85 per ton of CO_2. Comparing the social costs of carbon on a BAU trajectory and on a path towards stabilization at 550ppm CO_2 eq., Stern estimated the excess of benefits over costs, in net present value terms, from implementing *strong* mitigation policies in 2006: the net benefits would be of the order of $2.5 trillion. This figure – the Review claims – would increase over time.

This optimistic result has one important caveat though: "innovation driven by strong policy will ultimately reduce the carbon intensity of our economies, and consumers will then see reductions in the prices that they pay as low-carbon technologies mature".

III.iii Policy recommendations derived from the Review

The Stern Review recommends a series of policy measures to face the climate change problem: in the long run, there must be a way to reduce GHG emissions that is *mitigation*; in the short run, there should be *adaptation*. In both sets of policy measures, the government plays an important role through taxing, regulating, providing information and public goods, and financing the poor.

Mitigation

According to the Review the policy to *reduce* emissions should be based on three elements: carbon pricing, technology policy, and removal of barriers to behavioral change. It is emphasized that policy frameworks must deal, among other things, with interactions with a wide range of *market imperfections*.

With respect to carbon prices the idea is to establish an appropriate price on carbon –through tax, trading or regulation – so that individuals and businesses are led to switch away from high-carbon goods and services, and to invest in low-carbon alternatives. But to be efficient, this price must be a common *global* carbon price. However, investors and consumers must believe that the carbon price will be maintained into the future and credibility takes time so Stern proposes a period of transition of 10 to 20 years to reach the time when carbon pricing is universal and is automatically factored into decision making. In this transitional period – Stern argues – it is critical that governments consider how to avoid the risks of locking into a high-carbon infrastructure, including considering whether any additional measures may be justified to reduce the risks.

Secondly, the development and deployment of a wide range of low-carbon technologies is essential in achieving the deep cuts in GHG emissions that are needed. While the private sector plays the major role in R&D and technology diffusion, it is very important a close collaboration between government and industry for stimulating the development of a broad portfolio of low carbon technologies and to reduce costs. Public spending on research and development (R&D) – Stern emphasizes – must be increased relatively to what has been in the past two decades when it has declined.

Moreover Stern argues that the scale of existing deployment incentives worldwide should increase by two to five times, from the current level at the time. Such measures – he says – will be a powerful motivation for innovation across the private sector to bring forward the range of technologies needed.

Stern considers that the lack of reliable information and the existence of transaction costs, and behavioral inertia constitute barriers that prevent energy efficiency measures to be effective. In that case regulatory measures could provide clarity and certainty. "Minimum standards for buildings and appliances have proved a cost-effective way to improve performance, where price signals alone may be too muted to have a significant impact" (Stern, 2006).

Adaptation

According to the Review the governments play an important role in providing a policy framework to guide effective adaptation by individuals and firms in four key areas: (a) High-quality climate information and tools for risk management; (b) Land-use planning and performance standards; (c) Long-term polices for climate-sensitive public goods, including natural resources protection, coastal protection, and emergency preparedness; (d) Financial safety net that is required for the poorest in society, who are likely to be the most vulnerable to the impacts.

IV. Nordhaus versus Stern debate

The Stern Review's debate had various angles and many participants. A thorough analysis of this debate was done at the time by Frank Ackerman (2007) among others. In particular the criticism of Nordhaus was dealt with, also, by the outstanding economist Kenneth Arrow (2007). For the purpose of our analysis we present here, the background for this debate, the basic elements of the Nordhaus critique, Stern's own arguments and, finally, the "crucial" discussion on the discount rate between the authors above mentioned. Three basic aspects of the debate are involved: how expected damages were estimated; how uncertainty is treated, and the discount rate.

IV.i Background

Before Nicholas Stern was appointed to do the economic inquiry that was eventually known as the "Stern Review", there had been some global models for analysing the evolution and predictable impacts of climate change and global warming on earth's social and economic life, and deriving from it some policy recommendations to cope with it.

Even before the famous James E. Hansen's Statement before the US Senate Committee on Energy and Natural Resources hearing, called "The Greenhouse Effect: Impacts on Current Global Temperature and Regional Heat Waves" in June 1988 (Hansen 1988), there was a not less famous work called *Changing Climate, Report of the Carbon Dioxide Assessment Committee*. This was published in 1983 by the National Academy Press and edited by the chairman of the Committee, William A. Nierenberg. It collected the works of several scientists evaluating Climate Change, among which there are two chapters by William D. Nordhaus, and two other colleagues of him.

Nordhaus has been the leading economist of the University of Yale, in New Haven, U.S.A., for *General Equilibrium* models dealing with Climate Change. His modelling on energy can be traced as far back as 1973. The initial relevant work done in the seventies was his energy model of 1979 for the US energy sector where he tries to determine the prices of energy resources, for an *efficient* use of those resources (called "efficient prices"). The investigation was oriented towards establishing the time pattern of the efficient use of the energy resources assuming that those resources – which are scarce – have a royalty attached, that increases over time with the market interest rate. The difficulties the study finds in trying to adapt economic theory to real world facts – for instance the assumption of competitive oil markets that yield competitive oil prices versus actual oil prices determined by some degree of monopoly in the real oil market – leads the investigation to formulate the actual question of "what is the chance that global environmental effects will appear as a result of unrestricted market forces?" In answering this question Nordhaus concludes that "we are probably heading for major climatic changes over the next 200 years if market forces are unchecked". He, therefore, proposes a "carbon tax" as the *most efficient* control strategy (Nordhaus, 1979). The existence of non-competitive markets brings about some degree of uncertainty which adds to that inherent to the costs of new technologies estimates. It is, therefore, recognized that the validity of the results in this type of models is restricted by the very optimistic assumptions that there are no significant impediments for the action of market forces (Nordhaus, 1979).

In the 1983 report, the chapter by Nordhaus and Yohe presents a world probabilistic model for estimating CO_2 emissions as influenced by major uncertain variables or parameters. The technique utilized is called "probabilistic scenario analysis". The model is a highly aggregated model of the world economy and energy sector. The main equation is a multi-input production that related Gross National Product to labour, fossil fuels and non-fossil fuels inputs. The so called "key uncertainties" included in the model are, the rate of population growth, the availability and cost of fossil fuels, the productivity growth rate, and some others. The important findings in this model are "odds are even whether the doubling of carbon dioxide will occur in the period 2050-2100 or outside that period... it is a 1-in-4 possibility that CO_2 doubling will occur before 2050 and 1-in-20 possibility that doubling will occur before 2035" (Nordhaus and Yohe, 1983, p. 94). This chapter includes the projected CO_2 world's emissions and its rates of growth from 1975 to 2100, all of which are meaningless by now. The chapter by Ausubel and Nordhaus is a review of projections of CO_2 emissions and concentrations for 2100, which depend mainly on energy consumption levels and the substitution of fossil fuels for other energy sources, made by various experts including Nordhaus himself. Except for the recommended use of a tax on carbon-based fuels as the most efficient policy to stabilize or even reduce CO_2 emissions, the study does not go any further, since there is no analysis of Climate Change economic impacts or costs.

Nordhaus' "DICE" model is presented in 1992 (Nordhaus, 1992). It is called DICE for a Dynamic Integrated Climate Economy model. "The model is an optimal-growth model for the world economy. It is designed to maximize the discounted 'utility' or satisfaction from consumption subject to a number of economic and climatic constraints. The global economy is assumed to produce a composite commodity. The composite economy is endowed with initial stock of capital and labour and an initial level of technology and all industries behave competitively. Each country maximizes an inter-temporal objective function identical in each region which is the sum of discounted utilities. Population growth and technological change are exogenous. There is no need for international trade since the outputs of the different countries are perfect substitutes".

One important feature of this model is that it is assumed that "GHG emissions can be controlled by increasing the prices of factors or outputs that are GHG-intensive". The presentation also says that the model can be interpreted either as an optimizing framework or as an outcome of idealized competitive markets. It is assumed that the public goods nature of climate change is "somehow overcome in an efficient manner. That is, it assumes that, through some mechanism, countries internalize, in their decision making, the global costs of their emissions decisions".

The important conclusions from this version of Nordhaus' model results are that "an efficient strategy for coping with greenhouse warming must weigh the costs and benefits of different policies at different points of time...Estimates of both costs and damages are highly uncertain and incomplete...In terms of damages... the impact of climate change coming from a 3°C rise in global mean surface temperature...is estimated to be a about 1.3 of output for the global economy" (Nordhaus, 1992).

As an improvement of the DICE model, a new model called RICE is presented in 1996, by Nordhaus and Yang. The name stands for Regional Integrated model of Climate and the Economy. This is described as a regional dynamic general equilibrium model of the economy which integrates economic activity with the sources emissions and consequences of greenhouse-gas emissions and climate change. By disaggregating into countries the model analyses different national strategies in climate change policy. The model asks how nations would in practice choose climate-change policies in light of economic trade-offs and national self-interests for reductions of GHGs. In the RICE model the world is divided into 10 regions, each is endowed with an initial capital stock, population, and technology. Of these three variables capital accumulation is determined by optimizing the flow of consumption over time.

From to the results of the model there are some basic conclusions. The most important one is that the model estimates the difference between cooperative efficient policy and the non-cooperative policy. This latter is one in which countries maximize their economic welfare taking policies of other countries as given. "This implies that small countries whose climate change policies have little effect on their own economic welfare, will have little incentive to reduce emissions while the largest countries will have greatly attenuated incentives to engage in costly reductions in CO_2 emissions" (Nordhaus, 1996).

The results of the model indicate that the stakes in controlling global warming are *modest* in the context of overall economic activity over the next century. The estimates indicate that losses from global warming will be in the range of 1 to 2 per cent of global income over the next century. According to the model successful cooperation would lead to net gains, but the failure to cooperate is unlikely to lead to economic disaster over the next century.

In *Roll the DICE again: Economic Models of Global Warming* by Nordhaus and Boyer (1999) the authors made a detailed description of Nordhaus' general equilibrium world models built until then and they run a new version of DICE. The model called RICE-99 estimates damage functions for both the world and by region and sector. The results seem to be of the greatest importance: "The results differ markedly by region. The impacts (of a 2.5°C global warming) range, from a net benefit of 0.7 per cent of output, for Russia, to a net damage of almost 5 per cent, for India. The global average impact is estimated to be 1.5 per cent of output, using projected output weights and 1.9 per cent of output using 1995 regional population weights". "Current projections of RICE-99 indicate that total warming in an uncontrolled environment will be slightly below 2.5°C around 2100. Our estimate is that damages are likely to be around 1.9 per cent of global income using 2100 output weights. The damages for the US, Japan Russia and China are essentially zero over that time frame, assuming that catastrophic scenarios do not materialize. Europe, India and many low income regions appear vulnerable to significant damages over the next century", (Nordhaus and Boyer, 1999).

We see that as early as 1979 Nordhaus was aware of the need to have free market forces *under control*, in order to prevent a major "climatic change" over the next two centuries, if they were *unchecked*. The policy measure for "control" he proposed then – and became eventually his basic policy instrument all along his writings – was a *carbon tax* that would induce consumers and producers to switch from fossil fuels' energy to other sources of energy. For Nordhaus this carbon tax was the most efficient policy, which means *optimal* in Pareto's terminology. However, in the same analysis, he recognizes one big problem in his model which was – and still is – the assumption of perfect competitive markets, that introduces some degree of uncertainty on the validity of, at least some of, its predictions.

IV.ii Nordhaus on Stern

Shortly after the Stern Review was made public, Nordhaus published an article commenting on this Review mostly in a critical way (Nordhaus, 2006).

He starts by stressing how large in size the results of Stern projections were with respect to the estimates of losses from climate change damages, in terms of global GDP, under the BAU trajectory: "the *Review* estimates that if we don't act, the overall costs and risks of climate change will be equivalent to losing at least 5 per cent of global GDP each year, now and forever. If a wider range of risks and impacts is taken into account, the estimates of damage could rise to 20 per cent of GDP or more". These results – says Nordhaus – are especially dramatic when contrasted with those from "earlier economic models that use the same basic data and analytical structure", which one might presume are mainly those of Nordhaus himself. More to the point, Nordhaus states that those earlier models' results led to "efficient or optimal policies to slow climate change [that] involve modest rates of emissions reductions in the near term followed by sharp reductions in the medium and long term". This is what he calls "climate-policy ramp".

Nordhaus critical points are essentially these: first, "...while I question some of the Review's modeling and economic assumptions, its results are fundamentally correct in sign if *not in size*"; second he criticizes that the Review is not an academic study since it was not peer reviewed, therefore it should be viewed as a *political* document; and third, the most important, "....the Review's radical revision arises because of an extreme assumption about discounting. Discounting is a factor in climate-change policy –indeed in all investment decisions – which involves the relative weight of future and present payoffs... The Review proposes using a social discount rate that is essentially zero. Combined with other assumptions, this magnifies enormously impacts in the distant future and rationalizes deep cuts in emissions, and indeed in all consumption, today. If we were to substitute more conventional discount rates used in other global-warming analyses, by governments, by consumers, or by businesses, the Review's dramatic results would disappear, and we would come back to the climate policy ramp described above".

Besides these critical comments Nordhaus points out only one of Stern's policy measures which he apparently endorses: "the Review argues that it is critical to have a harmonized carbon tax or similar regulatory device both to provide incentives to individual firms and households and to stimulate research and development in low-carbon technologies. Carbon prices must be raised to transmit the social costs of GHG emissions to the everyday decisions of billions of firms and people".

IV.iii Stern's arguments

Oversized predictions and policy

If you compare Stern's projections of GHG emissions under the BAU trajectory shown in Figure 2 in Section III and the one from the current OECD's projection shown in Figure 1, Section II, you don't see much difference. Look at both graphs at the point of year 2050, and the only difference you'll notice is that while for Stern there will be still some GHG emissions from Land use, for the OECD there will be none, the estimated emissions from Land use per year are the difference between the two graphs, it is very little and based on different assumptions. So, Stern's GHG emissions projections were not particularly *oversized*. Therefore, the problem comes from other results of the Stern Review's model, those referred to the relation between global mean temperature increase and damages costs, both resulting from climate change.

At this point we must recall the strongest of Stern's prediction regarding global warming: "Under a BAU scenario, the stock of greenhouse gases could more than treble by the end of the century, giving at least a 50 per cent risk of exceeding 5°C global average temperature change during the following decades. This would take humans into unknown territory". In other words, in the extreme case, that is, over 5°C of increase in average global temperature, we could not even assess the magnitude of the damage involved, much less the costs in this future, beyond 2100.

But even at temperatures not as high, Stern clearly points out: "the monetary impacts of climate change are now expected to be *more serious* than many earlier studies suggested, not least because those studies tended to *exclude* some of the most uncertain but potentially most damaging impacts. Thanks to recent advances in the science, it is now possible to examine these risks more directly, using probabilities". The question of probabilities is put, therefore, at the center of Stern's analysis, so he uses the model called PAGE 2002 that takes into account "the range of risks by allowing outcomes to vary probabilistically across many model runs, with the probabilities calibrated to the latest scientific quantitative evidence on particular risks". Stern's projections of global temperature increases and monetary losses from climate change are presented within range of probabilities.

It is important to emphasize on some aspects regarding Stern "oversizing" costs and damages from climate change. Indeed, the expected damages and their costs in terms of GDP resulting from Stern model are higher than those which other models predicted before, in various ways and for various reasons. These are, in particular with respect to GHG concentration and global temperature increase: (1) the probability of reaching a higher level of GHG concentration in the atmosphere by 2050 and 2100, (2) the chance that this higher concentration leads to reach higher global temperature levels before previous estimated times and (3) the consideration of amplifying feedbacks in the climate system from climate change.

This probable new scenario of climate change has a higher than predicted monetary impact in all countries in terms of damage costs, with developing countries suffering even more than the average. Stern explicitly states that his model's results in monetary terms are even worse, when incorporating three factors, other models did not: (1) non-market impacts costs; (2) amplifying impacts costs and, (3) appropriate weighting of the unequal distribution of damages form climate change, for poor countries.

Therefore, the policy actions that Stern proposes have these characteristics: immediate starting, strong and including a wide variety of measures in which the role of the state is indispensable. This contrasts to what Nordhaus had proposed all along his studies which was a single policy: *a carbon tax* to increase *carbon prices*. And, by the way, this policy is not excluded in the Review itself.

Uncertainty and the discount rate

We have seen so far that Stern dealt with risks and uncertainty by means of probability, but Nordhaus refers to uncertainty linked to the discount rate in his critique: "A further unattractive feature of the Review's near-zero social discount rate is that it puts present decisions on a hair-trigger in response to far-future contingencies. Under conventional discounting, contingencies many centuries ahead have a tiny weight in today's decisions.

Decisions focus on the near future. With the Review's discounting procedure, by contrast, present decisions become extremely sensitive to uncertain events in the distant future".

To begin with let's see what Kenneth Arrow says in that respect: "Critics of the Stern Review don't think serious action to limit CO_2 emissions is justified, because there remains substantial uncertainty about the extent of the costs of global climate change, and because these costs will be incurred far in the future. However, I believe that Stern's fundamental conclusion is justified: we are much better off reducing CO_2 emissions substantially than risking the consequences of failing to act, even if, unlike Stern, one heavily discounts uncertainty and the future...Two factors differentiate global climate change from other environmental problems. First, whereas most environmental insults – for example, water pollution, acid rain, or sulfur dioxide emissions – are mitigated promptly or in fairly short order when the source is cleaned up, emissions of CO_2 and other trace gases remain in the atmosphere for centuries. So reducing emissions today is very valuable to humanity in the distant future....Second, the externality is truly global in scale, because greenhouse gases travel around the world in a few days. As a result, the nation-state and its subsidiaries, the typical loci for internalizing externalities, are limited in their remedial capacity...Thus global climate change is a public good (bad) par excellence. Cost-benefit analysis is a principal tool for deciding whether altering it through mitigation policy is warranted. Two aspects of that calculation are critical. First, it has to be assumed that individuals prefer to avoid risk. That is, an uncertain outcome is worth less than the average of the outcomes. Because the possible outcomes of global warming in the absence of mitigation are very uncertain, though surely bad, the uncertain losses should be evaluated as being equivalent to a single loss greater than the expected loss" (Arrow, 2007).

Frank Ackerman from the Global Development and Environment Institute, at Tufts University in the USA is a little more prolific in his opinion about Stern's discount rate. He argues to begin with that, in selecting the appropriate discount rate for long-term public policy decisions we must distinguish between two elements: one is the rate of pure time preference which is the discount rate that would apply if all present and future generations had equal resources and opportunities and the other is a wealth-based component, reflecting the assumption that future generations will be richer than we are. In the Stern Review, the discount rate, r, is the sum of these two parts in the equation, $r = \delta + \eta g$, where, δ is the rate of pure time preference, g is the growth rate of per capita consumption, η is a parameter that determines how economic growth affects the discount rate. Stern estimates that the growth of per capita income will average 1.3 per cent a year and sets $\eta = 1$. Thus, Stern's discount rate is: $r = 1.4$ per cent (Stern, 2006, Ch.2).

Nordhaus' critique is in fact centered on Stern's value for δ, the discount rate that would apply if all generations were equally well off. Stern, while accepting the philosophical arguments for treating all generations equally, observes that there is a small, but non-zero, probability that all future generations will not exist. The probability of humanity's extinction is assumed to be 0.1 per cent per year. It means that pure time preference is therefore set equal to 0.1 per cent (Ackerman, 2007).

The choice of a particular δ pure time preference rate is an *ethical* question, involving the value placed on the intrinsic well-being of future generations, independent of income. Stern favors a much lower value than other economists, but the choice – says Ackerman – is not a matter of technical analysis. So in order to quantify an ethical perspective that respects and validates the future, it is essential to set pure time preference close to zero. Regarding the choice of the second parameter, the exact value of η is not crucial to the general conclusions, *i.e.*, that the benefits of active, immediate mitigation outweigh the costs.

Finally, Nordhaus argument that discount rates should match current interest rates is for Arckerman a *mistake*, because it is grounded in abstract theories of perfect markets, not in reality. Ackerman concludes that markets are imperfect in countless ways.

V. Conclusions

Despite that liberal and neoliberal economists seem to have repeatedly won the theoretical and political battle since the seventeenth century against state interventionist economists, most developed countries have reached the level of development they enjoy today and could get out of economic crises, thanks to strong state policy measures.

Free market may be considered self-regulating – and market oriented policies as first best – under very limited circumstances, which are very unlikely to exist in all countries, at all times, like perfect competitive markets, full information, etc. Actually what is more probable to exist is a situation of many *market failures*, when some of these conditions are not fulfilled by economic reality in any given country at any given time. More over when they are not met at the same time, that is, when there are, for example, externalities, public goods, imperfect competitive markets, incomplete information and principal-agent problems simultaneously, as in the case of pollution in general and climate change in particular.

Whatever the extent of market oriented policies carried out between 1988 and 2005 they did very little in solving the GHG emissions problem, called Climate Change. Nicholas Stern pointed out in his Review, in 2006 after eighteen years of IPCC foundation, that Climate Change was "…the greatest and widest-ranging market failure ever seen" (Stern, 2006). Stern also called for a "major change" – as opposed to a marginal one – in GHG reductions which, as all major changes in the economy must be led by the state in each country case.

In the so called Stern Review debate, Nordhaus' criticism only reveals the weakness of his own argument for a free-market policy, which is the set of free-market assumptions that does not hold in any real economy.

References

Ackerman F., 2008, "Carbon Markets and Beyond: The Limited Role of Prices and Taxes in Climate and Development Policy", *G-24 Discussion Paper Series*, No. 53, December, United Nations Conference on Trade and Development.

Ackerman F., 2007, "Debating Climate Economics: The Stern Review vs. Its Critics" Report to Friends of the Earth-UK, July.

Arrow, K., 2007, "The case for mitigating greenhouse gas emissions", *Real-World Economics Review*, no.45.

Arrow, K. J., 1951,'An Extension of the Basic Theorems of Classical Welfare Economics', in J. Neyman, (ed.), Proceedings of the Second Berkeley Symposium on Mathematical Statistics and Probability, Berkeley, CA, University of California Press, 507–32.

Bergson, A., 1938, "A reformulation of Ceratin Aspects of Welfare Economics", reprinted in Arrow and Scitovsky (eds) *Readings in Welfare Economics*, Irwin, Homewood, Ill., 1969.

Bator, F. M. 1958 "The Anatomy of Market Failure", *The Quarterly Journal of Economics*, 72 (3), pp. 351-379.

Chang, H-J, 2003, *Globalisation, Economic Development and the Role of the State*, Zed Books, London.

Chang, H-J, 2002, Kicking away the Ladder, Anthem Press, London.

Debreu, G., 1954, "Valuation Equilibrium and Pareto Optimum", Proceedings of the National Academy of Sciences, reprinted in Arrow and Scitovsky (eds.) *Readings in Welfare Economics*, Irwin, Homewood, Ill., 1969.

Duval, R., 2008, "A Taxonomy of Instruments to Reduce Greenhouse Gas Emissions and their Interactions", OECD Economics Department Working Papers, No. 636, OECD Publishing, http://dx.doi.org/10.1787/236846121450

Foley, D., 2006, Adam's Fallacy, Harvard University Press, Cambridge MA

Franckx, L. and A. D'Amato, 2009, "Environmental policy as a multi-task principal-agent problem", *Working Paper Series no. 2003-12*, Energy, Transport & Environment Catholic University of Lovaine, Faculty of economics and Applied economic sciences, Center for economic studies, November.

Furman, J., M. Porter and S. Stern, 2002, "The Determinants of National Innovative Capacity", Research Policy, No. 31, pp. 899-933.

Hansen, J.E., 1988, "The Greenhouse Effect Impacts on Current Global and Regional Heat Waves". Statement presented to the U.S. Senate Comitte on Energy and Natural Resources, June 23, 1988. NASA Goddard Institute for Space Studies, N.Y.

Haščič, I., et al., 2009, "Climate Policy and Technological Innovation and Transfer: An Overview of Trends and Recent Empirical Results", OECD Environment Working Papers, No. 30, OECD. http://dx.doi.org/10.1787/5km33bnggcd0-en

Hepburn, C., 2010, "Environmental policy, government, and the market" Oxford Review of Economic Policy, Vol 26, No. 2, pp.117–136.

Intergovernmental Panel on Climate Change (IPCC), 2011, web link for history: http://www.ipcc.ch/organization/organization_history.shtml

Intergovernmental Panel on Climate Change (IPCC), 2007, *Climate Change 2007*, Fourth Assessment Report of the Intergovernmental Panel on Climate Change (AR4), R.K. Pachauri and A. Reisinger (Eds.) IPCC, Geneva, Switzerland, pp. 104.

Intergovernmental Panel on Climate Change (IPCC), 2001, *Climate Change 2001: Mitigation*. IPCC, Working Group III. Ch. 7 "Costing Methodologies", Cambridge, UK, Cambridge University Press, pp. 451-498.

Intergovernmental Panel on Climate Change (IPCC), 2000, IPCC Special Report Emissions Scenarios, IPCC Working Group III, IPPC, Geneva, Switzerland.

Intergovernmental Panel on Climate Change (IPCC), 1996, *Technologies, Policies and Measures for Mitigating Climate Change, IPCC, Technical Paper I*, WMO UNEP, Geneva, Switzerland.

Kaldor, N., 1939, "Welfare Economics propositions and Interpersonal Comparisons of Utility", The Economic Journal vol. 49, no. 195, pp. 549-52, reprinted in Arrow and Scitovsky (eds) *Readings in Welfare Economics*, Irwin, Homewood, Ill., 1969.

Kindleberger, Ch., 1973, *International Economics*, Irwin, Homewood, Ill.

Laffont, J.J. and D., Martimort, 2002, The Theory of Incentives. The Principal-Agent model, Princeton University Press, Princeton, NJ

Nordhaus, W., 2006, "The 'Stern Review' On the Economics of Climate Change" Working Paper 12741, National Bureau of Economic Research, Cambridge, MA.

Nordhaus, W., 1992, "The 'Dice' Model: Background and Structure of a Dynamic Integrated Climate Economy Model of the Economics of Global Warming", Cowles Foundation Discussion Paper No. 1009, Yale University, New Haven, Conn.

Nordhaus, W., 1991, "An Inter-temporal General Equilibrium Model of Economic Growth and Climate Change", in Energy and the Environment in the 21st Century, J. W. Tester, D. O. Wood, and N. A. Ferrari (eds.), MIT Press, Cambridge, MA.

Nordhaus, W., 1979, The Efficient Use of Energy Resources, Yale University Press, New Haven, CT, USA.

Nordhaus, W. and J. Boyer, 2000, Warming the World: Economic Modeling of Global Warming, Cambridge: MIT Press.

Nordhaus, W. and Z. Yang, 1996, "A Regional Dynamic General-Equilibrium model of Alternative Climate Change Strategies, The American Economic Review, v.86, no.4, pp.741-765.

Nordhaus, W. and G. Yohe, 1983, "Future Carbon Dioxide Emissions from Fossil Fuels," in National Research Council-National Academy of Sciences, Changing Climate, Report of the Carbon Dioxide Assessment Committee, National Academy Press, Washington, D.C.

Organisation for Economic Co-operation and Development, 1999, Action Against Climate Change: The Kyoto Protocol and Beyond, Paris, OECD publications.

Robinson, J., 1962, "Review of H.G. Johnson's Money, Trade and Economic Growth", Economic Journal September, LXXII, 287: 690-2

Robbins, L., 1938, "Interpesonal Comparisons of Utility" The Economic Journal, vol. 48, no. 192, December, pp. 635-641.

Roll, E., 1974, A History of Economic Thought, 4th Ed. Irwin, Homewood III.

Schatzki T. and R.N. Stavins, 2012, "Using the value of allowances from California's GHG Cap-and-Trade System", Analysis Group, August.

http://www.analysisgroup.com/uploadedFiles/Publishing/Articles/Value_Allowances_California_GHG_Cap_Trade_System.pdf

Schumpeter, J.A., 1966, History of Economic Analysis, Oxford, University Press, London.

Stern, N., 2007, The Economics of Climate Change, the Stern Review, Cambridge UK, Cambridge University Press.

Stern, N., 2006, The Stern Review on the Economics of Climate Change, H.M. Treasury, London, UK, October.

Stiglitz, J.E., 1991, "The Invisible Hand and Modern Welfare Economics" Working Paper No. 3641 National Bureau of Economic Research, Cambridge, MA, March.

Szatzschneider W and T. Kwiatkowska, 2008, "Environment & Principal-Agent approach", Riskmathics. http://www.riskmathics.com/files/PODCAST/Environment-Principal-Agent-approach-Wojciech-Szatzschneider.pdf

World Meteorological Organisation (WMO),1986, "Report of the International Conference on the assessment of the role of carbon dioxide and of other greenhouse gases in climate variations and associated impacts"

www.ingramcontent.com/pod-product-compliance
Lightning Source LLC
Chambersburg PA
CBHW081505200326
41518CB00015B/2386